To David

With Love,
Your Family
and Friends

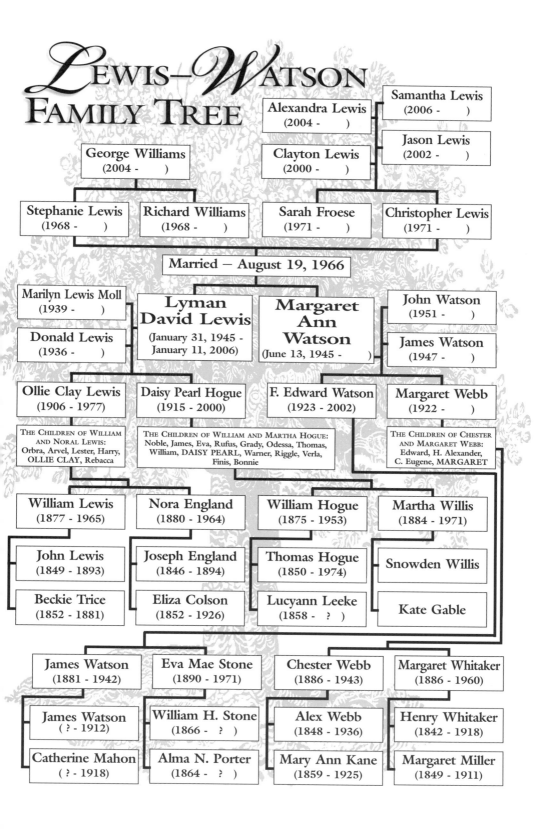

LEWIS–WATSON FAMILY TREE

Samantha Lewis (2006 -)

Alexandra Lewis (2004 -)

Jason Lewis (2002 -)

George Williams (2004 -)

Clayton Lewis (2000 -)

Stephanie Lewis (1968 -)

Richard Williams (1968 -)

Sarah Froese (1971 -)

Christopher Lewis (1971 -)

Married — August 19, 1966

Marilyn Lewis Moll (1939 -)

Lyman David Lewis (January 31, 1945 - January 11, 2006)

Margaret Ann Watson (June 13, 1945 -)

John Watson (1951 -)

Donald Lewis (1936 -)

James Watson (1947 -)

Ollie Clay Lewis (1906 - 1977)

Daisy Pearl Hogue (1915 - 2000)

F. Edward Watson (1923 - 2002)

Margaret Webb (1922 -)

THE CHILDREN OF WILLIAM AND NORAL LEWIS: Orbra, Arvel, Lester, Harry, OLLIE CLAY, Rebacca

THE CHILDREN OF WILLIAM AND MARTHA HOGUE: Noble, James, Eva, Rufus, Grady, Odessa, Thomas, William, DAISY PEARL, Warner, Riggle, Verla, Finis, Bonnie

THE CHILDREN OF CHESTER AND MARGARET WEBB: Edward, H. Alexander, C. Eugene, MARGARET

William Lewis (1877 - 1965)

Nora England (1880 - 1964)

William Hogue (1875 - 1953)

Martha Willis (1884 - 1971)

John Lewis (1849 - 1893)

Joseph England (1846 - 1894)

Thomas Hogue (1850 - 1974)

Snowden Willis

Beckie Trice (1852 - 1881)

Eliza Colson (1852 - 1926)

Lucyann Leeke (1858 - ?)

Kate Gable

James Watson (1881 - 1942)

Eva Mae Stone (1890 - 1971)

Chester Webb (1886 - 1943)

Margaret Whitaker (1886 - 1960)

James Watson (? - 1912)

William H. Stone (1866 - ?)

Alex Webb (1848 - 1936)

Henry Whitaker (1842 - 1918)

Catherine Mahon (? - 1918)

Alma N. Porter (1864 - ?)

Mary Ann Kane (1859 - 1925)

Margaret Miller (1849 - 1911)

Table of Contents

Chris, David, and Stephanie
1976 - Chicago

Introduction

This project began at the mid-point of my father's illness, with the idea that collecting a few of his life stories from friends and family would make him smile and would be meaningful to him. I had read a book by a man (a friend of someone I worked with) who had the same kind of brain tumor as my father's and his daughter had done something similar for him. Little did I know how this effort would grow and take on a life of its own.

I began by collecting stories from friends and family through email. The stories were far more beautiful than I could have ever imagined—some funny, some moving. Some were even accompanied with a picture. I read each story over and over, shedding many tears in the process. Unexpectedly, I learned a great deal about my father through the stories, many things about him I had never known. I learned what a great athlete he was as a teenager, how he had inspired and influenced so many people, and the big and little ways that he helped those in need. Through all the different perspectives represented in the stories, I started to see a *whole* person, not just a father through a daughter's eyes. I also saw that he had an important purpose in his life, which was to nurture and lead the communities of people who were so dear to him, and he so perfectly fulfilled his purpose.

The stories were not only helpful for me, but I began to see they were helpful for others too. Many of the authors mentioned how beneficial it was for them to express their thoughts and memories of my father. It helped them to process the situation and felt good to contribute something. One of my work colleagues read an initial collection of the stories and when she was finished, she came to me with tears in her eyes and tissues in hand. The book was deeply touching to her and caused her to think hard about her own life.

I originally compiled the stories in a scrapbook and gave it to my father when our family took a vacation together three months before his death. While he struggled to commuicate through words then, it was clear that he understood. After the trip, my grandmother read the stories to him, the two of them sharing memories and many tears.

Through this process, I had also realized that a scrapbook was not enough. As the collection of stories came together and I saw the amazing picture of my father's life that it created, I recognized that this book would help my son and my brother's children to know their grandfather, and I wanted them all to have copies. For me, one of the saddest parts of my father's illness has always been that his grandchildren will not remember him (or at least not remember much), as the oldest of his now five grandchildren was only five years old at the time of his death.

David Liverett, a graphic artist and owner of Chinaberry House, graciously offered to put the book together so that we could make multiple copies. I expected photocopied pages bound with staples—I had no idea it would turn out as it did! David added so much creativity and insight to the book. He put together a draft of the book that we displayed at my father's funeral. I never dreamed the book would generate the interest that it has, but we soon became inundated with requests for copies.

It certainly has taken a community to produce this book and I am thankful for the help of everyone involved—Martha Duncan and David Coolidge for distributing the requests for stories; David and Avis Liverett and Tammy Burrell for turning it into such a lovely book; my brother Chris, for digging out most of the photographs; and my mother for finalizing all the pieces and eventually running with the project. And of course, my deepest thanks to all the authors—this book is what it is because of each one's loving contribution.

As I wrote in my own story in the book, my father was truly a light in the world and my hope is that even though he is gone, his light will continue to shine through this book.

Stephanie Williams
Denver, Colorado
Jauuary 27, 2006

This really is David Lewis in 1946.

From the Beginning...

*W*hen I was growing up, the "facts of life" were never really discussed, just "hinted at," and I was very much into the subject when my Mother told me Aunt Pearl was going to have a baby. However, I immediately decided something must be terribly wrong with my understanding of the process to have a baby because my Aunt Pearl was not "that kind of woman" and after all, Uncle Ollie was a preacher!!!! So... perplexed was I on the entire subject of the new baby on its way. I decided that after the child was born (this had to be a miracle child to my way of thinking, it just *had* to be) I would decide how this whole deal came about but for the time being I just wouldn't let on that I knew what I thought I knew! During the pregnancy it seemed that was all the talk every time the family got together and I could tell Marilyn was getting a little jealous of "the new baby" getting all the attention. My Dad, who loved Marilyn dearly, decided the same thing and one evening made a point of discussing the coming event with Marilyn to get her idea about the situation. She told Dad she really wasn't happy about the whole thing but had decided that if it was a baby girl, it would be okay and they would keep it. At this point Dad inquired what Marilyn's plans were if the baby should be a boy! She looked him square in the eye, with her little hands on her hips and informed Dad that should such a disaster happen, "I will flush him down the commode!" That precious baby boy was born to a big sister who *mothered*

beyond imagination; she loved him dearly and was very protective of that baby brother. Dad many times offered to take David home with him since he was a boy and Marilyn let him know beyond a doubt that he had misunderstood her earlier, she wanted a baby brother all the time!

David has meant much to me all of his life. Remember his long curls when he was a toddler? He just always looked prettier than the rest of us...like the special child I had

David in 1950

predicted all along. When my Dad died, David and Margaret were serving as interim pastors at Tanner Street Church of God and they were with me when the last minutes of my father's life arrived. David stood beside my dad telling him it was okay to go to the sweet singing Dad declared he could hear in the distance. David encouraged him to walk toward that bright light that only Dad could see. He and Margaret Ann stood there beside me, Mother, and Michael and ministered to Dad in the sweetest, most gentle way you could ever imagine. My dad looked at me one last time with the sweetest smile and went to rest eternally. The process was so precious and I looked at David and said, "Thank you so much." In the hallway about thirty minutes later, David informed me that Uncle Lester, my dad, was the very first person he had ever seen die. I realized that the ministry David had given to my dad and my family was not something he had *learned* but it came from his heart; the kind, sweet, gentle heart of Lyman David Lewis. What a blessing!!! I am so proud he is my cousin!

— Shirley Lewis Bohannon

David in 1956

*O*n December 31, 1944, Uncle Ollie preached at First Church of God in East Prairie, Missouri. He had been asked to fill the pulpit because our pastor, Rev. W. E. Reed, had resigned as pastor, after accepting the pastorate of the Arrow Heights Church of God in Anderson, Indiana. To give a little bit of background, Daddy was in business in East Prairie, Missouri, and had been for several years. In late 1944, he decided to go into business with Uncle Ollie and Uncle Lester in Sikeston.

On December 31, 1944, at the close of the evening service there was a New Year's Eve party at the church. Uncle Ollie and Aunt Pearl, Donald, and Marilyn attended the party. After the party my brother, Edward, and I rode to Sikeston with them, because we were to enroll in school in Sikeston. Mother and Daddy decided that it would be better for Edward and me to enroll as early as possible, because they weren't planning to move to Sikeston until later in the month. Aunt Pearl was pregnant with David, and I was fearful that it would put extra work on her with our being there. But we felt at home, and the next day or so Uncle Ollie took us to Sikeston High School to enroll us. Edward was thirteen and I was eleven; he was in eighth grade and I was in seventh grade, but our classes were held in the high school. That evening, Uncle Ollie took us over to Grandma and Grandpa's hotel. They managed the Jefferson Hotel in Sikeston. We stayed with them until Mother and Daddy and the rest of the family moved to Sikeston.

Of course, we were at every service and function at the Tanner Street Church of God, so we were privileged to be with family a lot, which was wonderful. When David was born, I thought he was so cute and precious. I loved babies, so I was very thrilled when I learned that mother was expecting a baby in November. Glenn was born nine months after David, so they were close in age. My brother, Ray, and Donald were close in age, as were my sister, Donna, and Marilyn.

I loved our Lewis "get-togethers" every Christmas. What wonderful times we had, getting to be with our cousins, aunts, and uncles, and Grandma and Grandpa. The gift-exchange was so exciting for me. We couldn't wait for Grandma to come to our house a few weeks before Christmas, so that we could draw names. We really looked forward to that. I remember that one Christmas Uncle Ollie and Aunt Pearl made movies of our "get together." I don't remember the date, but I believe that it was at Uncle Hubert's business location. I have often wondered if those movies are still around.

Upon retiring from the ministry in 2004, my husband, Don, and I began attending The Church at the Crossing in Indianapolis, where David and Margaret are very highly regarded. It has been so good to see them in church and to hear of their work in missions. I saw David in January of this year. He was sitting a few rows up and to the right of me. I went to him and wished him a Happy Birthday. He was soon to leave on a mission trip to Africa; Margaret was already in Africa at the time.

David in 1962

David, we love you and are so very proud of you and all that you have been and all that you have done for God throughout the years. You are an inspiration to us and to our children and grandchildren. You were only nineteen years old when Grandma Lewis left this earth and went to Heaven, but I know that she is rejoicing because of the way you have lived your life in surrender and obedience to God.

We love you!
Don and Nonie Tawney

How David Got His Name

I can't swear that I really remember this. But I heard the story so many times that the night my new baby brother was named is a vivid one in my mind.

You have to understand that David wasn't just another baby joining a family. In many ways, his birth was a symbol of hope to our family. He arrived in the last months of World War II—as the horrendous siege that had gripped the entire world in a sense of dread for years was giving way to the possibility of peace. People were beginning to believe there could be a future, after all. So, Don's and my parents dared to plan for their own bright possibility...a third child.

It was Dad who wanted another child while Mom was determined to limit the size of her brood. Having been born ninth in a succession of fourteen kids, she'd received little attention from her own mother and had looked to her older sister, Viola, for mothering. Then, when she was just five, her world was shattered; her beloved Viola married and moved away, disappearing from her daily life. Small wonder Mom intended her life to be different. She vowed to have the time and energy to mother her children, to have financial resources adequate for their needs. (She and Dad were married in 1931 during the Great Depression). So she considered their family complete when she gave birth to me, the second child, a girl, to make a matched pair with her son, her first-born, Don. Obviously, Mom's determination had melted away when confronted with Dad's hope. So it came to pass that Mom delivered her third January baby. Earlier that month, Don and I had our birthdays; he turned nine and I was six years old. The year was 1945.

David barely made it in January; he was born on the very last day of the month. Amazingly, Mom and Dad had not settled on a name. How my parents could have not known what they wanted to name the baby, I don't know. But they couldn't bring their infant home from the hospital without a name on his birth certificate. David was the only one of the three of us delivered in a hospital. Don and I were born at home. So, on an evening soon after the baby was born, I accompanied Dad to the evening meeting of the Men's Brotherhood of the Tanner Street Church of God. I don't think

15

David Lewis, Marilyn Moll, and Don Lewis - June 2005

they met at the Tanner Street location because at that time, there was only a sanctuary with two small anterooms on either side of the choir loft; it was a barebones building with no place to serve a meal. Whatever the setting, I remember being abruptly hoisted to stand in a chair at a long table where I delivered, with gestures, the little *saying* my dad had rehearsed with me.

1) Momma had a baby,
Tiny little thing,
I bet I could put him
Through a rubber ring.

2) Ain't he awful ugly?
Ain't he awful pink?
Just came down from heaven?
That's a lie, I think.

3) My Momma told me
another great big lie.
My nose ain't out of joint
That's not why I cry!

4) Nasty, cryin' baby
Takes my place in bed.
I'm gonna take a drumstick
And beat 'im over the head.

16

Of course there were loud laughs. I was a bit confused about whether the men were laughing at, or with me, but I was promptly retired to the sidelines while Dad requested each man to submit a name for his new son.

The little slips of paper were taken to Mom in the hospital. Together, she and Dad combined two of the suggestions: *Lyman* and *David*. Lyman Dame, who owned a feed and seed store in downtown Sikeston, had suggested his own name. The name *David* was submitted by Hubert Keasler, husband of Dad's only sister, Rebecca. David was Hubert's brother.

From the moment I heard the name David, I loved it. By age six, I'd heard the wonderful Bible story of the boy David slaying Goliath the giant. His was a valiant name. And it seemed as beautiful to me as my new baby brother (*I never "hit 'im over the head with a drumstick" — or anything else. Not that I was such a peaceful child. I just never thought my blue-eyed, blonde-curled brother deserved any such assault*). I was so enchanted with the name that when I was given a "boy" doll for Christmas, I named it David. And later in my adolescent fantasies of marriage and family, David was the name of my imaginary son. "David" means "beloved." When I learned that, I never considered another name for Bill's and my first son – he's David.

— Marilyn Moll,

Dear David,

*Y*our name brings such a flood of memories. At Tanner Street Church of God in Sikeston in the 1960s, you were our Adonnis. All of the girls (seven or eight years your junior) were madly in love with you. Of course, we were far too shy to tell you. You walked in the room and we giggled. You said, "Hello," and we swooned. You were the heartthrob. You were handsome and smart, kind and sophisticated, athletic and polite. You were every mother's dream for a son-in-law. Then, the bottom fell out of our world. You married Margaret and broke all of our hearts. We wanted to not like her, but that was impossible. She was so much what we wanted to be.

All those giggling girls finally grew up and found our Adonnis to marry. Thank you for setting the standard so high.

— Jan (Hitt) Slattery Callen

September 6, 2005

*T*here are going to be many fine stories about David because he is simply one of the most wonderful persons in the world. But the two stories I have to share took place when David was only fifteen months old and it came to me by telephone from my mother a few days ago.

My father and mother moved back to Portageville, Missouri, just after World War II in February of 1946. Sometime in the last 1940s when David was only fifteen months old, Uncle Ollie, Aunt Pearl and my father went to the Missouri State Ministers' Meeting. David had been left in the care of my mother along with her three boys. Mom was thrilled to baby-sit David because Aunt Pearl rarely left her family. After the first night and early the next morning there was a knock at the door. When Mom opened the door a neighbor stood there holding David in his arms. He had found him out beyond the

David in 1946

sidewalk about to cross the street. Apparently David had awakened very early, opened the front door, pulled a stool up to the screen, lifted the screen door hook, walked out to the sidewalk, and was about to cross the street. Mom guessed that David, after awakening, found himself in a strange place and set out for more familiar surroundings. She said to me that kind of intelligence in David was a portent of things to come.

When Wednesday night came, Mom went to midweek service taking her three boys and David. Dad had left a new convert in charge and that young novice had chosen a very unusual passage to be read for consideration and comment. She said the text from the King James Version read as follows:

Now King David was old and stricken in years; and they covered him with clothes, but he gat no heat. Wherefore his servants said unto him, Let there be sought for my lord the king a young virgin; and let her stand before the king, and let her cherish him, and let her lie in thy bosom, that my lord the king may get heat. So they sought for a fair damsel throughout all the coasts of Israel, and found Abishag a Shunammite, and brought her to the king. And the damsel was very fair, and cherished the king, and ministered to him: but the king knew her not. (I Kings. 1:1-4)

After the new convert read the text he asked for comments. Mom said she sat there with her boys and David in an almost paralyzed state. She was fighting hard to keep from laughing and wondered what anyone would say. Sure enough, Sister Dockery, an older dear saint, and favorite of both the Hogues and the Lewises, stood to make her comment. Mom could hardly believe it, but waited breathlessly to hear what Sister Dockery would say. She responded by saying, "King David was anemic like me." Mom thought she would burst out with anguished laughter. She said that Uncle Ollie, Aunt Pearl, and Dad would have kept a straight face, but she never could when things got that funny in church meetings. She knew she had to get out of there quickly so she gathered David up in her arms as if he needed instant attending to, and ran out of the building where she laughed and laughed. She said to me, "Lyman David saved the day for me."

I am fairly sure these two stories will be unusual, but they are true.

Love from your cousin,
Oliver Hogue

Remembering

Since we moved away from Sikeston when David was only about three years old, my memory of him is very limited. I do recall, vividly, the bright red design imprinted on his face, the result of falling on a hot floor furnace. Also, I remember his blonde curls — quite "angelic" in appearance.

— Donna Lewis McGee

When I entered the Lewis family, David was still a lad. He had done something clever, I don't remember what, and was asked "Was that original?" and he replied, "No, I made it up!"

— Jeanne Reese

1956 . . . I lived with Aunt Pearl and Uncle Ollie while my dad was overseas in the Philippines for the Air Force. David was in the 6th grade at the same school where I was in first grade. He was also a school safety patrol and I was very proud that this important student was my cousin. He would push me on the swingset at school and ride bicycles with me to the library and the little Quick-Pick store on the highway. At home, he let me follow him around and he showed me where all the red squirrels lived and helped me *harvest* cotton from the field behind the house so I could see how it grows and experience picking it. He and I got together with cousins and neighborhood friends and put together a *play,* complete with costumes. However, the costumes were mostly old clothing from somewhere in storage and we all ended up getting impetigo and itched like crazy!

Marilyn was engaged to Bill at that time and such a beautiful young lady. I wanted to grow up just like her. I was so very proud to be the flower girl at her wedding in August of 1957.

— Taza Keene

ecause of the age difference, we certainly were not close growing up, although I remember different vague scenes taking place there in the Lewis family room in Sikeston. I especially remember a holiday night when Holly Bailey and I wanted to be in there with David, Danny Lopp and Greg Bailey. They were playing pool and the other guys didn't want us girls around, but David indicated it was okay and that seemed to settle the matter.

Without any doubt David is the best of both parents. He embodied the compassion and caring of Aunt Pearl and the humility and practicality of Uncle Ollie. David has always been "David" no matter what the event or situation. I adored that about him.

> Sincere love,
> Tanya Hogue Shupe

April 8, 2005

ou probably don't know me. You were a couple of years behind me in school, but I grew up in Sikeston knowing your dad and Lewis Furniture through my parents. I will always remember one Thanksgiving morning in the mid-1950s. When my mom got up early to put the turkey in the oven, the burner dropped out from overuse. Mom informed Dad of the problem. Dad waited until about 8 AM and called your dad and said, "We have a problem." Your dad asked my dad, Cecil Boyer, to meet him at the store. They picked out a new stove and your dad even came to our house to help hook it up. We had a good, but a little late, Thanksgiving dinner. You can't get that kind of service anymore.

I heard about your situation from my good friend at Kingsway Furniture and wanted to let you know you are in our prayers as well as many other Sikeston folks. We wish you the very best.

> — Larry Boyer

I have only known David and Margaret since retiring in Anderson in 1991 and attending Park Place Church, but I have had a few occasions to share some of our mutual family ties from before he was born. David has been on our daily prayer list since discovery of his physical problem and will remain so.

The Hency, Lewis, and Hogue families have numerous ties and evoke many nostalgic memories, although most are before David's time. I will list a few. David's parents, Ollie, and Pearl (Hogue) Lewis, were my pastors where I was born and grew up in Vanduser, twelve miles north and west of Sikeston, Missouri.

My family is listed as "charter members" in the Vanduser Church of God. It was founded in 1918 and was a thriving congregation preceding the Sikeston church. Even before I was born in 1925, my eldest brother, E. Raymond Hency, was an early pastor of the Vanduser church after the founding pastor, Edna Delay, left to start other churches in Illinois. At the age of twenty-one, Raymond was the last student in the county to qualify to start high school in Vanduser and he pastored the church as a high school student. I have a 1933 photo of the Vanduser church family taken when David's parents were pastors there. I count about 115 in the photo. Ollie and Pearl and at least twelve members of my extended family are in it.

My mother, well qualified by giving birth eleven times, attended Pearl at her birthing of David's brother Don. She reminded me of that when we worshiped with her in Sikeston several years ago.

David's father baptized me, as a kid, in a ditch "swimming hole" east of Crowder, Missouri, after I got saved in a revival meeting. We were close friends with the Hogue family when they lived about a mile south of Vanduser. I spent lots of Sunday afternoons visiting and playing with the Hogue boys near my age. Our favorite game was swatting the swarming wood bees in the air from the barn lot, using a stick. We competed by counting the number each could kill in a certain amount of time.

David's Aunt Verla was very close friends with my sister, Grace. His Aunt Bonnie was my age and in the same class in school. I have a photo of that class. I had a boyhood crush on Bonnie, but I doubt she knew it. I also had crushes on Dorothy Jean Edwards, Georgia Puckett, and Pauline

Kirby, but they didn't know it either.

David's grandpa Hogue was quite an inventor. I remember his cotton picking bicycle, the envy of every cotton picker who saw it. The wheels were cut from a large log, hooked together by a wooden frame with a discarded cultivator seat. He straddled, seated, and pushed himself along without having to bend or crawl on his knees to pick two rows of cotton.

Raymond later became pastor to David's uncle, Grady Hogue, in Illinois and sang in a quartet with him. Grady gave me a photo of the quartet. Raymond also performed Grady and Margaret's wedding.

Of course, there's the marriage of Jeff Lockhart, grandson of Grady, to Nancy Beard, granddaughter of my brother Raymond, another Hency-Hogue relationship.

1959 at Culver Military Academy

There's probably more, but that's enough. I hope David and other members of the family get some mild chuckles.

— Warren W. Hency, Jr.

Dear Family,

I have some fond memories of times spent in Sikeston, Missouri, with David Lewis during my pre-adolescent years. I remember being impressed with David's athleticism. During the fall, we were out in the side yard next to the carport with a football. I was amazed how far David could punt the ball, deep into the large yard across the street. It was probably so impressive to me because it was the first time I had seen, up close, someone do that skill. I think whenever I played neighborhood football back home in Columbia, I would try to emulate the form I observed from David that fall day in Sikeston.

Of course, I also remember David's entertaining, comical nature. He could do a mean

David Lewis – Moonlight Madness in 1963

Donald Duck voice. I tried to do it, too, with only limited success.

In Mammaw Pearl's later years, she often called me "David." I assume since David is her youngest and tallest son and I am her oldest and tallest grandson, this was a natural *faux pas*. I just remember feeling honored to be mistakenly called "David" by Pearl.

Thank you for asking me to share these memories.

Love, Reese Clayton Lewis

PICTURED ON PAGE **25**: *1962 Dexter Regional Champs – Sikeston High School (left to right): Gary Miller, David Lewis, Ken Davis, Benny Heuiser, Tim Garner, Bill Munger, Paul Cannon, Bill Ryan, Ronnie Bloemer, emcee Sherell Summit of Dexter, and Ed Berry.*

Basketball Practice

August 23, 2005

My Uncle David was thirteen when I was born, so I'm guessing this memory must have been from when I was somewhere around five to eight years old, making him a late teenager or an early twenty-something. As a kid, one of my favorite things to do at Tanner Street Church of God was to bounce the red rubber balls in the old gym. The basketball goal was pretty much out of my reach. Well, occasionally I would get lucky and bounce one in or, through divine intervention, actually give one a big enough heave to go in that sky-high hoop. Most of the time, I was content to work on dribbling those bouncy balls off the glossy, super-polished linoleum tiles. I loved the huge racket it made, noise bouncing off the walls and down the corridor.

One time, David came in wearing a sleeveless uniform with a real leather basketball and started shooting hoops while I was playing at the other end of the court. He was tall and lean and moved so fast with long, graceful strides. When he leaped for his jump shot, I remember thinking his sneakers must have been magical for him to go so high. The squeak of his shoes on the floor, the clang of the ball off the rim and swoosh through the net were much cooler sounds than the monotonous "boing, boing, boing" of my rubber ball. I stopped to watch, entranced.

David in 1963

I moved down to his basket to get a closer look. He had a routine: foul shots, lay-ups from one side and then the other, short jumpers, hook and perimeter shots. I don't remember the order, but he seemed to be able to shoot from anywhere; and when he missed, he thundered by me to scoop up the rebound or tip it in. Just about the time I thought I had seen enough to decide he was the best basketball player in the whole world, he went over to the corner and pulled the door open into the gym. The room was so small (still is) that it stuck a couple of feet into the court. David stood behind it and shot jumpers explaining to me that he needed practice shooting over tall guys where he might only see the basket at the last second. Time after time he sprung into the air releasing high arcing shots. I remember a good number of them swished through.

In retrospect, it may have been that day's display of physical prowess that first raised him to hero status in my eyes, but it has been his grace and incredible capacity for love and acceptance throughout his life that holds him there today.

— David Moll

David vs. Goliath

I want to pick up on David's life in the summer when he enters the ninth grade. I had just recently returned from Anderson College with my small family – infant son Reese, and Jeanne. I also returned with considerable pride regarding my own athletic experiences in football, track, and semi-pro baseball.

I immediately found myself compelled to be David's coach and tutor in sports. He was involved in Babe Ruth baseball. After pitching several no-hitters in Little League, he was a promising, and later outstanding, pitcher in the league. I felt the need to mentor him much more than I am sure he wanted or needed.

Midwest Plains Regional Babe Ruth TOURNAMENT

CHAHINKAPA PARK
Wahpeton, North Dakota
August 12 - 13 - 14, 1960

IOWA - MISSOURI - KANSAS - COLORADO - MINNESOTA - NORTH DAKOTA

Sikeston Babe Ruth was a hotbed of talent. My story is about how, after being one of the best two pitchers in the league, he was omitted from the All-Star Team on the grounds that he went to church camp for a week at an inopportune time, so the All-Star coaches thought.

David had pitched two wins in Sikeston's march to the state championship but then was omitted when they went to the regional. They subsequently won the regional and qualified for the national finals. Perhaps I was more bothered by this than David.

The team subsequently finished second in the U. S. and came home triumphantly. Immediately, they decided to stage an All-

28

Star game between the two best squads of the league – a celebration of sorts, staged for the local folks.

The luck of the draw put all three of the pitchers of the national team on squad along with most of the sluggers, with David pitching for the opposing team. It looked like a mismatch and it was. David shut down the triumphant, cocky team and showed them what good pitching would do to good batters. He showed a rare moment of satisfaction regarding this and next year was not omitted from the All-Star team.

This was not the end of my attempts to coach David from the sideline in his football and basketball careers in high school.

His grace in managing my ambitions for him taught me much about my desires to influence my son's athletic career. As usual, I learned my lesson slowly and regressed several times, but in the end David taught me that pride comes before a fall – especially when it is vicarious.

— Don Lewis

MISSOURI STATE CHAMPIONS – SIKESTON, MISSOURI

Left to Right, front row: Don Abies, 2nd base; Mike Garner, bat boy.
2nd row: Tim Spears, shortstop; Allen Wernecke, outfield;
Paul Polley, pitcher and outfield;
Joe Godwin, outfield; George Hale, infield; Bill Munger, outfield.
3rd row: Des Becker, manager; Kenny Davis, centerfield; Travis Holland, outfield and pitcher; David Lewis, pitcher; Jack Sims, outfield; Tim Garner, pitcher and infield;
Bill Ryan, catcher; Ronnie Bloemer, infield; A. G. Davis, coach.

29

My Little Brother

by William G. Moll
September 11, 2005

I never had a little brother.
Until David Lewis came into my life.
It was his big sister, Marilyn, who brought us together.

In so many ways, I've "frozen" David in time.
I still see him as my little brother.

My earliest memory of him is as a nine-year-old.
When you're nine, your world is still fresh and new. You face each new day with a sense of anticipation, expecting only good things to happen. And they usually do.
Good things happen to those who expect them. David still *expects* good things to happen.

David in 1955 - 10 years old

His eyes. It's in his eyes – that expressiveness. They light up all the way to his heart.

In 1954, Marilyn and I were dating.
I'd come to the house on South Prairie Street to pick her up and more often than not it was David who opened the door to greet me.
And the eyes said it all.
Welcome.
Come in.
I like you.
Marilyn likes you, so that makes you okay.
Mom likes you. That makes you *really* okay!

And the smile! The smile came from even deeper inside him.
I still see him that way. Frozen in time.
Blonde hair. Butch cut. A smile larger than his face. Eyes aglow.
Anticipating something good – and fun!

I'd never had any idea what it might be like to have a "little brother."
David filled the role completely.
He loved to talk about sports. The whole family did.
O. C. seemed to live vicariously through every boy on every team.
"Coach Lewis" was always there. On the football field during practice.
Keeping score at the baseball park. At the scorers' table in the gym. Always
eager to talk about sports.

And David was such a natural.
Baseball. Football. Basketball. Track. They all were so effortless to him.
Or so it seemed.

Don – his *real* big brother — was both his role model and his coach in every
sport.
Sports came naturally to him, too. And he wanted to pass on the skills,
knowledge, strategies of every sport. Every game.

I didn't have that much to contribute.
Just encouragement. Marilyn and I were pretty good at cheering him on.
That's what an ersatz big brother and a real big sister could do.
We were naturals at being his cheering squad.

Today, when we're together I still see him as my "Little Brother."
We sit beside Colorado's Dillon Lake munching a sandwich, sipping iced tea
at the Yacht Club.
It's a sunny, breezy day.
Sunlight dancing like fireflies on choppy water.
Thunderheads building overhead.
We don't say much.
Just take in the beauty of the moment.
Just us.
It's a moment frozen in time.

Me and my little brother.
David.

I am about four years younger than David. We lived in Boulder, Colorado for a few years and left when I was twelve. We would come "home" (Sikeston) to visit Grandmother Lewis and would stay at "Uncle Ollie's and Aunt Pearl's." David was always good with me when we came even though I'm sure I was a pain in the butt. Pardon the colorful language but some of us are better with words than others.

One traumatic event that has scarred me for life was a day trip David and I took to St. Louis. We had moved back to Sikeston by this time and I was in junior high. We left early one Saturday morning in Uncle Ollie's Falcon station wagon. (What a ride! Now that was a *chick car!...not!*) We had a load of

David Lewis in 1963

Admiral window air conditioners that we were taking to Admiral for repair. We were picking up some new ones to bring back to the store. Now you must remember that David was an exceptional student in school and was really good in math. Well, he had a theory (how he came up with it I don't know but...) that if you count so many seconds and you didn't see a car you could pass *even if there was a yellow line.* You've got to picture this. Two teenage boys in a *hot* red and white Falcon station wagon with a *load* of worn-out air conditioners. David applied his theory, counted it down, and around a car we went. With the accelerator floorboarded I still think I could have outrun the thing! But there we went. We *finally, with great effort, got even* with the car we're trying to pass only to find out that the theory, having never been tested outside the laboratory, *was an utter failure!* Because what did we have looking at us but a big eighteen-wheeler! The only thing good about the Falcon was it had some brakes. David slammed on the brakes. Here came about four or five used air conditioners. I was trying to hold them back so they wouldn't displace *me* from the front seat. David whipped

Summer - 1963

it back behind the car *we were trying with all our might to pass...safe*. Now that was a *Depends* moment if there ever was one, but as was usual for me, I wasn't prepared. The moral of this true story is *smart* people *can* get you into trouble and never buy a *Falcon* car of any sort!!!

On the same trip, when we had done the air conditioner switch at Admiral, we decided to go to the St. Louis Zoo. We had a good time and had seen a lot of the animals. We were beside the Gorilla cage. An eight-to-ten-year-old boy was tormenting a Gorilla and you could tell by the look on the Gorilla's face that he was *not* a happy camper! All of a sudden this gorilla jumped down from his perch and as gracefully as a dancer came across the cage scooped up a handful of *gorilla stuff* and threw it at the little boy. David and I were in close proximity to the little boy, but because we were at this point so accident adverse *and* because the little boy accidentally warned us by *screaming* to his dad, as he hastily retreated,..."Watch out dad he's got more *stuff*,"...but for the grace of the good Lord we were not severely injured! Now that was a close call. Two close calls in one day was all I could handle. We gingerly returned home shaken by the trauma of the day!! Perhaps a little more color than you want, but a true story, so help me God! The truth hurts sometimes.

Thanks for this great idea and the chance to pass on *a good time* I had with your dad.

— Sam Keasler

David Lewis and Margaret Watson on a date in 1963

David and Margaret's Honeymoon in the Bahamas

Camping
1977

1971

Our Wedding Plans

*O*ne of the joys of being married to Craig is his family. And Craig
came with a lot of family. When Craig and I were engaged in 1994,
it quickly became apparent that most of our wedding guests would consist
of the Lewis clan. Coming from a Catholic upbringing, I brought my own
wedding prerequisite, primarily that we would get married in the Catholic
Church—no small thing for a member of the Lewis family rich in their
history in the Church of God. And so our wedding plans became not only
a marriage of two people but of two deep family traditions.

As Craig and I proceeded with our wedding plans at Holy Trinity

David and Margaret Lewis, Holy Trinity Church, Washington, D.C.
"Renewing our Vows" (August 1995)

Church, we picked our favorite priest to preside over the ceremony, Father.
Dick McHugh. Craig and Dick had a lot in common at the time, namely
the amount of time they had spent in India. And so it came to the point
where Craig and I began to plan the ceremony itself. It was a given that we
would want David Lewis to play a prominent role in the ceremony and that
we would sing the "Doxology." So we went to Father Dick and told him

about our desire to have David participate in the ceremony and he responded, "He can do the whole thing." Perhaps it was his Irish brogue or the ever present twinkle in his eyes that left us both speechless for a moment. For the uninitiated, a Catholic wedding is not official unless the priest pronounces the vows. I panicked and said, "But this needs to be official." He laughed and said that as long as he was there it wouldn't be a problem. We should design the ceremony however we pleased.

We wanted to honor all of the long-lasting marriages that would inspire us through the difficult times and provide a symbol of our promise made before God. And so this is how we came to have both David and Margaret Lewis lead our guests in a renewal of their wedding vows. My most vivid memory of our wedding ceremony was looking at our guests turning to each other, hand in hand, and repeating their wedding vows. There wasn't a dry eye in the place, ours included.

Thank you David and Margaret, for sharing your faith, your example of marriage, and your love with us all.

Love,
Cynthia and Craig Moll
7 October 2005

Margaret and David's wedding on August 19, 1966

The very first moment I beheld him my heart was irrevocably gone. Jane Austen

January, 2006

Dear David,

*H*ow can I choose just one or two stories to remember when there are nearly forty-five years between us? What about the year that you sent me a card for Valentine's Day from Indiana and I sent you the very same card from Kentucky? We were separated by miles, but not our hearts. Should I tell that I finished college in three years so we could get married since you insisted one of us had to be a college graduate before we could marry? We've had good and adventurous years. There's the "big trip" with the children and our mothers. Or could I choose to tell about the challenging moves we made, mostly moving the goods ourselves. Oh, the wonderful memories of our beautiful and loving children and our family stories. Then there were almost sixty countries we visited with hundreds of fellow travelers. And there is this year, our last year together when we knew for sure that God had His hand on us. This is the year that we have traveled with cancer. We've had quite a journey together these almost forty-five years – an adventure that I have been blessed to join you on.

But the story I want to share is the one about the first time I met you. It's just as Jane Austen wrote in *Northanger Abbey*, "The first moment I beheld him my heart was irrevocably gone." That's exactly the way I felt. In 1960, my family moved to Sikeston, Missouri, from the tiny little town of Clarkton, Missouri. It was a big and scary move for me to go from a town of 1000 to a city of 15,000. Could I really make the adjustment? Soon after arriving in June 1960, I began to hear about DAVID LEWIS. First of all everyone was talking about how intelligent you were. The girls were talking about how cute you were. The mothers were talking about how nice you were. It seemed that the whole place was talking about DAVID LEWIS. But the real talk that summer was about the Babe Ruth Team. They were awesome and DAVID LEWIS was the pitcher. The Babe Ruth Team was going to the World Series. Well, we didn't meet all summer even though there were just three doors and a street between our houses. I could see your bedroom window from our front door. I could watch you outside washing the car, mowing the lawn, playing ball in the driveway. My curiosity was high! We finally met at the famous Sikeston Cotton Carnival. My friend, Marilyn Conrad, took me and there we ran into you at the cotton candy booth. Marilyn introduced us, but I never said a word other than "Hi." You don't even remember meeting me, but I remember meeting YOU. I remember what you and Marilyn talked about. I remember you standing there so tall and handsome and athletic and intelligent just like everyone had said. Can that be almost forty-six years ago? You and Marilyn were making jokes and laughing and you butchered some Spanish to make her laugh. I just stood there. But it was in that moment that I

fell in love, just like the other girls in town, but I had this strange intuition that someday we would date. That was too funny for a shy girl just standing there behind her friend. I didn't know when we would date and there was no hurry, but you and I were meant to be. A little presumptuous I would say. But that's exactly what happened. Almost one year to the date of our first meeting we had our first date. It was on September 23, 1961 — a very special date that we celebrated for years.

I love you, DAVID LEWIS,
Margaret

September, 2005

*T*o my son-in-law, David:

Words cannot express what you have meant to me through the years. You always welcomed me into your home and made me feel like an integral part of your family. This included your extended family of parents, siblings, nephews, nieces, uncles, aunts, and cousins.

I have many happy memories because of your generous spirit which allowed me to be included in family events and family trips.

The greatest gift of our relationships has been the faith we share in the one true God – Father, Son, and Holy Spirit. Through the good times and the bad times our faith has brought us through.

Margaret Kathryn and David in Kenya, 2004

Bless you, my dear son-in-law and when all is done, may God receive you into His arms and say, "Well done, my good and faithful servant."

Your mother-in-law,
Margaret Kathryn Watson

41

Dad

*W*hich story about you do I choose? Let me start by saying that you are an inspiration to me with the manner in which you conduct yourself. You are honest, hardworking, love your work, willing to help, fun to be around, and always looking to further God's kingdom. You provided so much to me, Stephanie, and Mom that I want to do the same for my family.

You were always there willing to help me with any homework assignment. You seemed to love to give me a mini-lecture about the subject of my essays or research papers. You seemed to know everything and a good game of Trivial Pursuit proved it on many occasions.

I remember many special events that we have done together and as a family. I remember going camping where we made a campfire, roasted marshmallows for s'mores, and learned to play blackjack. We hiked the Canyon, went into caves, sailed a catamaran, rode on horseback, and marveled at the Red Woods. I remember you driving the van while pulling the camper and always leaning over to look out the window down the side of the mountain. It always made the rest of us nervous.

I learned to appreciate art and architecture from our many trips across the ocean. I certainly learned to appreciate all that we had from those trips as well, and to be concerned about the fortunes of others that don't have the opportunities that we have here.

I remember sitting down and having popcorn or a 5th Avenue candy bar watching the *Rockford Files* and *Cheers*. Or as a lifelong Cardinals fan trying to show interest in my beloved Cubs games during the summer. Or stopping by the neighbor's driveway after one of your mile runs to shoot some hoops with me. Or taking me out to play golf and teaching me the basic grip and swing.

I remember you performing the marriage between Sarah and me. You did a wonderful job and were beaming throughout the entire ceremony. I was honored that you were the one that married Sarah and me. That is probably the second best highlight of my memories of you.

But the first memory that always comes to mind is the day I was baptized. You came around back where I had changed out of the wet clothes and into the dry ones. You were waiting for me to come out and you stopped me so that you could give me a big hug. You looked at me

Front row: Jason and Clay
Back row: Chris, Sarah, and Alexandra with Margaret and David
Colorado, August 2005

and told me how proud you were of me and that you loved me. We weren't a very expressive family back then, so this was a very meaningful event and I could tell. I will always remember that look on your face.

Well, I love you too, Dad. I always will.

— Chris

Dear Dad

*Y*ou have given so much to me throughout my life, and one of your greatest gifts has been a love for learning. You have always been such a curious person. When I was a child, I thought you knew everything. You may have formally studied history and religion, but you have always known a great deal about many more topics than those. We called you our "walking encyclopedia" and joked that your brain was full of "trivia." When we took our "BIG TRIP" out west, you started off by stopping the van at every historical marker along the road–fortunately we got you to quit doing that or else we might STILL be on that trip!

There was one time–remember this?–when my awe of your knowledge got me into some trouble. I was in grade school in Richton Park and heard the kids at school talking about Walter Payton. I didn't know who he was, so that evening I asked you about him. You said matter-of-factly, "He's the

governor of Indiana and Illinois and he lives in a big governor's mansion on the border of the two states." Well, that sounded good to me – and of course, you knew everything so who was I to question! I marched to school the next day and announced to the other kids that "I" knew who

Walter Payton was – and I proceeded to tell them what you had told me. Needless to say, my classmates got a good laugh that day.

On a less mischievous note, I remember when I was in high school and had to write my very first term paper. You suggested that I choose the Oneida Community as my topic, which I did. That was the first time that I saw an assignment not just as something to simply finish for a grade but as an opportunity to learn about a part of the world and history I hadn't known. I loved researching and writing about Oneida. That love of learning continues as an important part of who I am and I thank you for helping to instill it in me.

There are many other things I've learned from you – discipline, love of other cultures, and exploring the world. I believe, though, that I've learned the most from you over the past few months, during this time that you've been sick. You have faced your illness with strength, grace, and even humor. You've rarely gotten frustrated or angry when most others would have. You have a sense of true peace and joy. It shows in your eyes. You have taught me that an illness like yours is a natural part of life and not a "bad thing" to be feared. You have faced your illness in the same way you have lived the rest of your life, and you are a role model to those of us who have experienced this illness with you.

Thank you for being my father. And thank you for being such a light in the world.

> I love you,
> Stephanie

For Better or for Worse

I don't remember dwelling on it much, but when I was young, I always assumed I would be married by the rabbi I grew up with in Houston. But then I met David Moll and I fell in love. After he asked me to marry him and he agreed to raise our children Jewish, the rabbi part did not really matter to me. I knew my rabbi would not perform a wedding ceremony if David wasn't Jewish—and I had no intention of asking him to convert. Oddly enough, I don't recall being too concerned about who was going to marry us. I don't even recall when, in the grand scheme of wedding planning, that David told me he had an uncle (also named David) who not only *could* perform our wedding ceremony, but *would*. I thought "Now how cool is that, to be married by your uncle?" So, without any hesitation, I immediately said, "Yes."

Many, many hours of heated discussions, tears, and turmoil followed my decision. How could I agree to this without ever having met him? How could I choose this uncle over an offer from a non-practicing, ex-rabbi, whom I had also never met? How could I be certain that he wouldn't start "preaching" and saying the "wrong" things in front of all my Jewish friends and family?

I could not explain how I knew in my heart that I had made the right choice. I had no doubt in my mind that Uncle David would be every bit as generous, open-minded, and loving as the rest of David's family. When we spoke to Uncle David about the kind of simple, non-religious ceremony that we wanted, he was very responsive to all of our wishes. He was warm and understanding. He accepted me and respected me and never once made me feel uncomfortable. He never questioned or criticized my opinions or beliefs. I knew that everything was going to be fine. And of course, it was. His kindness, compassion, and loving spirit even won over the biggest skeptics in my family. Our wedding was absolutely wonderful. And having Uncle David officiate made it all the more memorable.

That simple act of loving kindness, from David, was just one of the first indications of what a unique family I was lucky enough to be joining. I am truly privileged to experience the love and support that always comes from this wonderful group of uncles, aunts, cousins, and in-laws, that I now call my family, too.

I love you all,
Stephanie Moll

Don Lewis, Marilyn Lewis Moll, and David Lewis families in Colorado

Front row left to right: Jordon Moll, Don Lewis, and Vega Cain
Second row left to right: Craig Moll, Liam Moll, and Cynthia Moll,
Marilyn Moll, Stephanie Lewis Williams, Amy Green, Luna Green
Third row left to right: David Moll, Stephanie Moll, Danny Moll,
William Moll, and Richard Williams
Fourth row left to right: Margaret Lewis, David Lewis, Danielle Lewis,
Blake Lewis, Kathleen Cain Lewis, and Stephen Cain
Fifth row left to right: Reese Lewis

I first met David Lewis in the spring of 1966 at South House on the Anderson College campus. This beloved abode stood where Reardon Auditorium lobby is now located. David and Dan Yelton were roommates just down the hall from my room on the second floor. My roommate was Arnold Raymond from Homestead, Florida. On the first floor were several African-American students and I don't recall all their names but I remember Mervin Moss. He was the blackest black person I had ever seen. In the basement was the shower and a small area that served as a kitchen.

Avis and I have been close to David and Margaret for over thirty years. They were already a part of Truthfinders Sunday school class when we began attending and they were great at having parties at their house on Woodview Drive. One party was so crowded but Margaret managed to read the story "A Cup of Christmas Tea" and she gave everyone some tea to take away as we left. I think this was the first time I had ever seen a portable telephone and I remember during the evening David got a call and he walked out of the room with the phone. It seemed amazing.

I designed several covers for the Church of God youth magazine *Between Times* and once I created a tablet of commandments out of styrofoam to look like stone. It had five dating rules and David and Margaret posed for the cover standing at the front door pointing to one of the rules as the boy looked on before the date with their "daughter."

In 1994, Avis was on staff at the National Board of Christian Education and part of her job that year was to go to the International Youth Convention in Memphis. We traveled with Joe and Anita Womack and on the way we stayed in Sikeston, Missouri. We ate at Lambert's Restaurant. We started talking with the owner and asked if he knew David Lewis. As it turned out when we went to pay for our meal, the lady said it had been covered. We laughed and said that David Lewis was good for a free meal at Lambert's. We also visited both furniture stores while in town.

Our son Mark planned a surprise party for our twenty-fifth anniversary.

Warner Sallman's son, James Sallman, with David Liverett and David Lewis

It was held at David and Margaret's. It was a wonderful celebration with many of our friends attending. Our quest group was where we really got to know David and Margaret. They were in charge of putting the group together. The members included Jim and Rita Martin, Spencer and Sue Spaulding, David and Margaret, Jim and Deanna Edwards and Avis and me. We each gave our faith journey story and it was very interesting to find out more about our friends.

Several years ago we met David and Margaret in Chicago to see the Warner Sallman paintings and to meet Sallman's son. Actually Avis and Margaret went shopping while David and I enjoyed a lecture on the importance of Sallman's paintings of Christ.

When I moved to Anderson to attend college, I was amazed to learn how many people were related to others in the church community. After my first book was published, David's mother told David that they were related to the Liveretts. As I recall the connection, my uncle Andrew's wife's grandmother is a sister to David's great-grandmother. At this point, I am glad to claim him as a "shirt tail" relative. I only wish that I had known the connection back in the mid-sixties when we were living in South House.

I feel very fortunate to have had David as my friend for these forty years.

> With sincere appreciation,
> David Liverett

One of the personal highlights of my student experience at Anderson College was the opportunity to work with David when he was managing editor of the *Andersonian* and I was associate editor in 1965-1966. He was a junior and I was a sophomore, and we were both history majors. As you can imagine, we spent a good deal of time talking about history, but we never had a class together. But the thing that I remember most is not a serious academic moment, but one of those moments of mischief that we all engage in once in a while.

One Saturday morning, David and editor Bruce Reinhardt and I were working busily to finish the paper reasonably on schedule—something that didn't always happen. After finishing our work, we went to the dining room and had a leisurely lunch. Once we had finished, the four of us stacked our trays and consolidated all of our dishes on the top. The load was so heavy it took two of us to lift it. We ceremoniously carried it to the conveyor belt and watched to see what happened when it got to the kitchen. We thought it was very funny, but the poor student who was clearing the trays thought it was anything but funny. I saw him grab a piece of silverware and throw it back at the tray, about which time Bruce, David, and I skedaddled as fast as we could.

On a more serious note, David did his historiography paper on the causes of the Civil War and gave me a copy. Of course, he earned an A, and it provided me with a model I could follow when I took the same course my senior year. My success on that paper, which was on Charles A. Beard's economic interpretation of the U.S. Constitution, was very important when I started doctoral studies several years later. So in that sense, David helped model success, one student to another.

— Dr. Carl E. Kramer

I would think that there are too many stories I have about David, most of them quite humorous. I would imagine that the year I took a class that he was "professing" would be the one I remember most. In fact, it was probably the only time I ever saw that side of "Big Dave." I remember the class being a liberal arts seminar and as vague as the title was, my little brain thought it would be fun to take a class from David. After day one, in which I was challenged to write some sort of "paper" concerning the writings of Socrates, I realized I was in over my head. I usually required a Thesaurus since David's vocabulary contained words that were well beyond my understanding. "Just like Dad," I would think. For the most part, I stayed quiet and to the rear of the classroom. But, David being David, he would not allow any of us, especially me, to not participate. He would threaten by announcing that participation was a portion of your grade and I remember taking this threat seriously. However, now that I am older and wiser I have mused that David would not give such an easy grade. In fact, his class may have been one that challenged me the most. I received a "B" (barely) and was so proud of it. I went to David after grades had been posted and thanked him for his mercy. He looked at me and said that I should have tried harder and if I would have shown some effort that I could have achieved a higher grade. This point had been made to me by my father on more than one occasion but did not hit me like David's words. I think maybe hearing it from my "other Dad" was what did it. I cannot recite or recall many (okay, most) of the teachings of Plato, but I can tell you I will not ever forget the fourteen weeks I spent in his class.

— Andrew Duncan

Dear Margaret and all:

*M*utual friends have kept us up to date in recent months and, more particularly, in recent weeks about the state of David's health, always declining, and the strength of your care and support. I mentioned to friends that I should be feeling my age as one after another of my former students dies.

I carry around in my diary a list of one hundred and fifteen people who "did" their Ph.D.s with me, and there is David Lewis (1979), which means he was at Chicago in the turbulent years of the early-to-mid-seventies. It seems like only yesterday to me, and memories of him are vivid. I remember him working hard on the Chicago laity of one hundred years ago: how the same people were converted by Dwight Moody and moved to action by William Rainey Harper. They could never figure out why evangelism and action-reflection couldn't go together, and why the two had separate constituencies. I think David was always someone who could "bridge" between the two worlds.

I remember well a day at his school, and got occasional reports about his teaching, but I understood that his paralleled commitment to the "family business" also kept him tied to Sikeston. He served there well, and had his priorities in the right order.

It was good to hear of the family being gathered at his bedside; probably by now there's been one more grandchild added to the list. Now I hope that in prayerful concern you will be supportive to each other, and in the Christian hope by which he lived, you will all be sustained by the promises of God and your envisioning of David in the fulfilled resurrection life.

I hope our paths will meet from time to time. I am richer for the way and the times that David's and my paths met.

> God give you comfort, in Christ
> Warm regards,
> Martin E. Marty

53

*D*ear David,

In the seventeenth century one of England's great poets, John Donne, wrote these lines, "Do not ask for whom the bell tolls. It tolls for thee." I will miss you. I have known you since you were a small boy in Sikeston and watched the boy become a man. I am proud to have my name on your diploma. And I have some memories.

I met you for the first time when I came as speaker for the State of Missouri Young People's Convention in Sikeston which was being held over the Thanksgiving weekend about 1956. You were about ten years old. I had been invited by your mom and dad to eat Thanksgiving dinner with your family which included a considerable number of guests. I came a little late and the feast had already begun, and after I collected my meal, there was no place to sit. Your dad called across the room to you and told you to find me a place to sit. You asked me if I minded standing up and I said that it was no problem. Next you asked if I minded eating at your grandmother's sewing machine and that is where I ate. Thanks. You have always found a place for me in your life.

Another memory was a Sikeston visit when you were trying hard to make it on the high school football team. You were sitting on the bench during one of the games, just dying for the coach to put you in when he called your name to go in. You leaped from the bench, caught your foot in the water pipe and slammed into the ground breaking your arm. It was a bad day but you took it like a man, and like most of us it was not the only time you had to get back on your feet and play another day.

Your dad taught you many things, among them frugality, which was his passion and the reason he was able to share his wealth with many causes in which he believed. In one of my visits to Sikeston I came with Philip Cooper, who for many years was the Anderson College attorney, and we gathered in your living room to discuss the transfer of the major gift which made the O. C. Lewis gym possible. It was lunch time and your mom came out of the kitchen with sandwiches. Now Mr. Cooper was a Presbyterian and not accustomed to Church of God ways. After a quiet moment, O. C. called on Mr. Cooper to give thanks. This was a shock to our Presbyterian friend who was not ready for the invitation and hardly accustomed to being called on to pray but after some considerable throat clearing he began, "Dear God,...uh...ah...whereas we are about to have lunch and whereas...ah...and whereas in consideration of this food before us we hearby give thanks." I am glad you were not in the room. Later when your family drove to the campus for the dedication you told me that your dad was fearful that too much was being made of his generosity and did not want people to think you were "uppity." Furthermore, he was eager to downplay the importance of the event in the eyes of his kids. So, you drove your old car into a one-star hotel on the west side of Indianapolis and camped for the night. You were not impressed but we laughed about this many times. But, those of us who knew O.C. Lewis honored him for the Christian values to which he was passionately committed and I lived to see them in your own life.

Well, David, you and your lovely wife Margaret have been choice friends along the way. You now have moved on to a place prepared for you in the promises our Lord has made which is beyond our knowing. Your old college president is proud of the manner in which you have taught and blessed thousands of your students who carry you into the future in their hearts.

– Robert H. Reardon
President Emeritus

David Lewis joined the Anderson College faculty in the fall of 1978, while I was dean. I had known David primarily as a good man, one who held an excellent Ph.D. from the University of Chicago Divinity School. I worked to bring him to the full-time faculty. It quickly became apparent to me that here was the kind of teacher-model we desired to place before our students; here was a jewel of a man.

We talked candidly about his assignment and his *fit* during both my dean and president years. His preparation in church history and a number of areas was superb; he was uneasy about his more limited preparation in some of his teaching areas. We made changes in his course expectations. Later, to assure that David felt *right* about his fit, we changed his home base department to history. Also we asked him to carry some substantial administrative assignments.

David was a man with a keen sense of integrity, a remarkably strong scholar and teacher. I valued him so highly and was anxious to keep him as a vital and strong faculty member. I am so grateful he gave us those twenty years!

– Robert A. Nicholson
President Emeritus

Dear David and Margaret,

We will always be grateful for the series of gatherings you encouraged, guided, and nurtured over several months here in Anderson and out of Park Place Church. Your interest, easy leadership and delightful friendship made this a group Deanna and I could join with the ease not often found for persons who are so often thrust into leadership roles. We found in you and the other couples who gathered a comfort of Christian fellowship that was special in every way, from the shared stories, ideas, hymns, and refreshments, to the inner feeling of deep regard we received so generously from both of you over the months we met. We are deeply grateful for the memory of these times together.

On two occasions over the recent years, I have had the opportunity to be with Dr. Martin Marty of the University of Chicago. Most recently we had a couple of days together at Pepperdine University for a conference on Faith and Scholarship. Marty has on both occasions reflected on the two students who have made such a significant impression on him, and of course, one is L. David Lewis. (The other was Roger Hatch.) Marty spoke easily of his acquaintance and long-held regard for both David and Margaret. He brought up the matter of the acquaintance when, on the first occasion of our meeting, I told him I was affiliated with Anderson University. It was the unusual fact that he had a particular fondness for two students and that they were both alumni of Anderson that invited his comments, completely unsolicited by me.

The memory I will hold of our friendship and work together also must include those few but important occasions when we crossed paths as we did only a few months ago outside Decker Hall, when we took a few moments to catch up and to talk about the business that was calling you back to Sikeston more regularly. I believe I reminded you of the occasion I was a guest in the home of your parents and we spoke about the Sunday School lesson O.C. would be teaching the next morning at church. It was on tithing. He had rather firm ideas on that subject and on how a Christian should live his life from a business perspective, giving witness to all about his deepest commitments and most preciously held values. The home was, in my opinion, a setting for family comfort, but nothing was elaborate or ostentatious. It was the Lewis home. And I am sure that has something to do with the feeling we have always had when we have been privileged to be in your home across the years.

There have been those occasions when I have asked for your good advice and we have talked about common concerns across the years. In those times, common sense and a deep regard for all involved, and especially for the work of the church, seemed to be the guiding direction of your thoughts and your good counsel.

O.C., Chris, and David at Anderson campmeeting, 1976

I do sincerely hope we will have times for fellowship and shared memories in the future, and want to always assure you of our deep regard, love, and prayers. We admire you so very much for all you have brought to the cause of Christ, to your students and those whom you have served through Anderson University, and the work that has called you so many times to Africa and other places of service. You are both among the most remarkable and admirable persons we have been privileged to know and we send your our best wishes for God's peace.

Sincerely,
Jim and Deanna Edwards

I met David and Margaret years ago as a student at Warner Southern College. David was my professor in an ancient history course and I worked with Margaret in the school library. David was a sharp and compelling professor. His teaching totally turned me around from my typical response of dread to anything related to historical study to a new response of curiosity and pleasure at his way of teaching about the human experience. In that sense, of all my professors, he made the most profound impact on my life as a student. Margaret was the "sweetest" (and prettiest) employee in the library. Her quiet humor and open smile made the very mundane tasks I was assigned to be more tolerable. I had not known David and Margaret for long when my fiancé, Loren Clark, contracted leukemia. My two stories about David come out of that time period, 1974-75.

For periods of time, while Loren was being treated at M.D. Anderson Medical Center in Houston, Texas, I stayed with several local families. My usual practice was to stay at the hospital full-time and return to a home-base only occasionally. One late night I crept in quietly, collected my pile of mail and went to the restroom where I sat on the floor to open it. (It was the only place I thought I would not disturb my host family.) One of the many letters that had come was from David and Margaret. That letter included a $100 check. I broke down in sobs. That amount felt like $1,000,000 to me. It was so timely and such an expression of support and caring. Why did I weep? Their generous spirit had preceded the gift for so long that the "gesture" was simply a reminder. (Bathrooms are good places to cry—there is plenty of paper for "snottin' and bawlin'.") That brings me to my second story.

Earlier, late spring of 1974, I left Houston after many weeks there with Loren to return to Warner Southern College. That meant I had to leave Loren in Houston; even though he was doing well, that separation was traumatic. Loren had convinced me to return to the school to try to finish my studies so I could graduate with my class. It was three weeks before the end of the semester. Because of the work load involved, I was sleeping very little. I was writing papers for classes, one after another. Since I did not type at the time and was so overwhelmed, I requested help from Margaret who offered such a service at the school. When I went to pick up that paper from Margaret, what did I find? I saw David Lewis sitting there finishing up the job for me. I was astounded, dismayed, and overwhelmed. Here was a

David and his mother, Pearl Lewis Stafford

former professor of mine typing my paper for another professor of mine!

In these little windows into the past, David and Margaret overcame the distance between older and younger folks, between those with status and power and those without. They responded eagerly to meet need and hurt with compassion. Their humility, generosity of spirit, and passion for life and life together have impacted me in the deepest places to form the spiritual values that I teach and try to live out today. David, I just hope my life does some justice to your investments of love and wisdom. What a difference you have made in my life!

Sharon Clark Pearson
Associate Professor of New Testament
Anderson University, School of Theology

Dear David,

We are writing this just at the start of the 2005-2006 school year at AU. Though Ken no longer teaches, the week takes him back to the bit of nervousness he would feel at such a time until the first classes had met and the fall routine had been established. A special time for that was the fall of 1978 when I believe you and I were both starting in as new recruits and coming to the campus from other experiences in teaching, studying, and serving in the church. We got the usual pep talk from President Reardon and a bit of careful guidance from Dean Nicholson. We struggled to get our books installed in our cramped Decker Hall offices and to get to know an array of new fellow faculty members and then a host of students. We had to learn how to fit into the campus bureaucracy. It was good sharing a time like that with you. In the years that followed I admired your knowledge and teaching skills and your commitment to Christian service both in this country and abroad.

Then there were those wonderful Tri-S (Study-Serve-Share) trips that we took with a wonderful assortment of friends. Margaret was Girl Friday for a lot of those travels. It opened the world to us and to one another. We saw cathedrals and castles, rivers, fiords, and mountains. Remember when we almost got blown off the Cliffs of Mohr by the fierce winds? And we ate in all kinds of places. Do you remember the medieval dinner at a castle in England? Speaking of castles, do you remember staying at the castle in Spangenburg? Herbie could scarcely drive the bus into the gate with maybe an inch to spare on each side? Like children we trooped from one room to another inspecting each couple's digs. And there were the wonderful pastry shops Norm could ferret out. And always the wonderful camaraderie on the bus. Like the time on one very hot travel day when the people in the back of the bus were very uncomfortable. Martha Thompson handled that by taking off her blouse and folding it on her lap. Remember the very old kirk in Norway where we gathered for worship as Christians had done there for eons. Then there were the exciting sessions getting oriented for the trip. You gave leadership to some of these. More exciting were the picture parties afterwards. How blessed we have been to have these experiences and to have the caring of one another.

And it was good to serve together around Park Place. We are so grateful for your service there. Much love to you and Margaret and your family.

Your friends,
Arlene and Ken Hall

David,

*I*t was my special privilege to serve with you on the Anderson University faculty for a brief time in the Religious Studies Department and to serve on the Park Place Church Council under your leadership. You were always competent, well prepared, wise, and an inspiration to serve with and under. I consider it a great personal loss that our paths have gone in different directions in recent years, but I never questioned but that you were serving faithfully where God had called you

My prayers are with you and Margaret in these difficult days.

With affection and admiration,
Don Collins

May 25, 2005

Dear Dr. Lewis:

*G*reetings from Arcata, California—where the redwoods reach the sky! I have heard from my folks who attend Park Place Church of God, that you have been quite ill, and I wanted to let you know you have been in my thoughts and prayers. You might remember my folks, John and Betty Little. You were my professor for several classes at Anderson University including Church of God history and U.S. history. I later married Sterling Evans; you might remember him, also. He teaches U.S. history at Humboldt State University in Arcata. Sterling is more of a Latin Americanist and he tries so hard to teach some of the forgotten and terrible part of U.S. history, such as how Native Americans were treated. In fact, he edited an anthology dealing with that issue. I always tell him that your class was one of the first times I heard details regarding how Native Americans were treated. I always sing your praises. You were a super professor—and I always enjoyed each and every class!

I fondly remember the classes I took from you.
In Christ, Sheri (Little) Evans

*A*s David's successor at Overseas Council International, I have many happy David stories. I have often shared that, during the transitional period after I became president-elect of OCI but was still in Costa Rica, David was a prince as he worked with me on transitional issues. In fact, we spoke of writing a short book or a long article on "transitions that work."

David served OCI during a particularly difficult period in the organization's life. He bore a very heavy burden during those years and sometimes had to carry out his responsibilities thanklessly.

Once, we were speaking on the phone, he in Indianapolis and I in Costa Rica. He was calling to give me some very good news about an internal OCI decision that was going to have very little effect on his period in office but was bound to be great news for me as his successor. It was the second or third piece of such news that had arrived in just a couple of weeks.

Francis Tsui and David Wang with David Lewis

I said to him, "David, I can hardly believe all this is happening *now!* You've worked so hard and faithfully without the benefit of all this, and it's as though the table is now being set for me to waltz in and enjoy circumstances you never had."

David replied immediately, "David, that's exactly what I *want!* I want you to have that opportunity, and I'm overjoyed that it's happening."

This story represents just one of many opportunities I've had to glimpse and receive encouragement from David's integrity, character, and humility.

With great affection,
David Baer

When I knew of David's sickness, my wife Ri and I were traveling in the U.S. Never in my adult life did I cry for anyone on hearing of his or her illness. But I did for David. It shows the depth of friendship.

Though we are from the same denomination, I did not know David until he joined Overseas Council International as the assistant to the president and later became the president of that organization. I was then the principal (president) of Union Biblical Seminary. Our friendship grew as we met in different places. He along with Margaret visited us in Union, at Pune and also Shillong, our hometown. I had stayed in their home in Anderson and also in all the three houses where they lived in Indianapolis. I had been with them to many exotic restaurants of Indianapolis.

David was such an encouragement to me. He is gentle, patient and yet strong and wise. During our times together, we dreamed a lot of dreams about ministries and other things. One of them is to ride on a toy train to Darjeeling. I do not know whether we will ever be able to do this, but it will remain a sweet memory for me.

I saw David again in June 2005. Just last month in August, my wife and I were again in Anderson and visited him and Margaret. Both times, in spite of his sickness, I could see peace written on his face. It must be the peace of the Lord Jesus Christ. David, you speak once again to me and to many of us, my brother.

— Leaderwell Pohsngap, Shillong, India

Leaderwell, David, Margaret, and Ri - August 2005

Studying and Traveling

MAP OF THE WORLD
showing possessions of
UNITED STATES, GREAT BRITAIN,
FRANCE and GERMANY

the World

A Short History of the Civilization Group

*O*ur calendars indicate that it is "time" to celebrate Christmas once again. As we take time to reflect upon the blessings of the year, we especially count our times together as a "Civilization Group" as some of our most memorable. I thought perhaps it was "time" to write down the remembered history of this group. So here goes...

In May 1981, Dale and Linda Bengtson and David and Margaret Lewis spent a weekend in Chicago. During that weekend, we attended a Chicago Symphony concert, a play at the Blackstone, and went to the Art Institute. As we were coming home, we decided that we needed more *civilizing* events in our lives. That fall we invited persons we thought might enjoy art, music, history, to a discussion group at David and Margaret's. We decided to show the Kenneth Clark video series called *Civilization*, where he showed how the music, art, architecture, and history intertwined through the centuries. We invited about forty persons who attended the first meeting. By the third or fourth meeting, a group of twelve had become the "real" Civilization members. That group was Dale and Linda, David and Margaret, Jerry and Joann Burand, Margaret and Irv Arouh, Georgia and Gibb Webber, Larry and Sue Osnes. I believe Margaret and Irv brought the Burands in at the second or third meeting. As years passed, Larry and Sue Osnes were divorced and he moved away. Sue continued to be part of our group. At that time Sue Osnes brought Darlene Miller to become part of our group. Then Osneses were remarried and she joined him in Minnesota.

The group continued monthly meetings, first completing the viewing and discussion of the Kenneth Clark series, then choosing a variety of subjects to discuss. Other subjects were the Galway series of *Music in Time*, Bill Moyers *World of Ideas*, Joseph Campbell's *Power of the Myth*, the viewing of a John Phillip Sousa tape and part of some operas. This year we have discussed the Gail Sheehy book, *New Passages, Mapping Your Life across Time*. This was especially helpful to us as we retire and approach our *second adulthoods*.

We have traveled together, going to many parts of the world that we had only talked about—England, Scandinavia, Greece, Eastern European countries, and many European countries. Some of us went to Costa Rica.

Some went to Tahiti. We have gone to bed and breakfast homes in Madison, Indiana, and Amish country. We have gone to a Greek restaurant before going to Greece. Joann and Jerry have taken us on "mystery" visits. Over the last six or seven years, going to the state parks in October has become a tradition. We alternate between McCormick's Creek and Pokagan. We established other traditions through the last few years such as: The Christmas brunch, held at Bengtsons until this year, and now at Lewises, and the Thanksgiving dinner held at Arouhs. The Burands traditionally host a New Year's Eve party unless our travels take us elsewhere. It is good to have special times with special friends.

We have enjoyed both our learning and our social times. We have supported one another in our sad times, deaths of family members, divorces, operations. We have joined in celebration in weddings of our children and birthdays.

I finish this short history of our "Civilization Group" with my favorite scripture, found in Ecclesiastes, about *time*:

For everything there is a season, and a time for every matter under heaven:
> *a time to be born, and a time to die;*
> *a time to plant, and a time to pluck up what is planted;*
> *a time to kill, and a time to heal;*
> *a time to break down, and time to build up;*
> *a time to weep, and a time to laugh;*
> *a time to mourn, and a time to dance;*
> *a time to cast away stones, and a time to gather stones together;*
> *a time to embrace, and a time to refrain from embracing;*
> *a time to seek, and a time to lose;*
> *a time to keep, and a time to cast away;*
> *a time to rend, and a time to sew;*
> *a time to keep silence, and a time to speak;*
> *a time to love, and a time to hate;*
> *a time for war, and a time for peace;*
> *What gain has the worker from his toil?*

I have seen the business that God has given to the sons of men to be busy with. He has made everything beautiful in its time; also He has put eternity into man's mind, yet so that he cannot find out what God has done from the beginning to the end. I know that there is nothing better for them than to be happy and enjoy themselves as long as they live; also that it is God's gift to man that everyone should eat and drink and take pleasure in all his toil. I know that whatever God does endures forever; nothing can be added to it, nor anything taken from it; God has made it so. That which is, already has been; that which is to be, already has been; and God seeks what has been driven away. —Ecclesiastes 3:1-15

The Civilization Group at McCormick's Creek State Park:
Jerry Burand, Georgia and Gibb Webber, JoAnne Burand, Darlene Miller, Margaret Arouh,
Dale Bengston, David, Linda Bengston, Irv Arouh, and Margaret

So we have this *time* together. We are pleased that we do. We are thankful that this Christmas, 1995, that we have had almost fifteen years together and we're looking forward to many other times. Friendship has truly been a precious gift.

Merry Christmas, 1995
Linda and Dale Bengtson

David and Margaret,

We want to celebrate, again, the privilege of being co-founders of the Civilization Group with you. Even though the writing is ten years old, it speaks to the real issues of life. David has always listened and acted on his great knowledge of history and civilization.

Joseph Campbell, Bill Moyers, the Scripture, and David Lewis have all spoken to us in profound ways that will always be with us. We love you.

Dale and Linda Bengston
September 15, 2005

Dear David and Margaret,

*A*s I write this on a beautiful September afternoon, I smile when I think of all the ways our paths have intertwined. Since all of us are sixty now (or in Jim's case, 62) these memories do become more precious.

David, you and I were freshmen together at Anderson College in the fall of 1963. Both of us happened to be in the same English class which met at 8 AM three days a week and at 7:30 AM two days. I remember that you and a couple of other guys sat on the front row and you always seemed to be an alert student at that hour. Some of us never ventured that close to the front and had to try desperately to stay awake!

We all moved to different places after college, but in July of 1985 we shared one of those delightful Tri-S trips led by Norm Beard. Our traveling group was a choir which went to the Orient – Japan, Seoul, Hong Kong, and mainland China. You took Stephanie and Chris along, and we took Kurt. When we sang and visited at the Church of God school for girls in Tokyo, we observed that many of those giggling schoolgirls wanted to have their pictures made with Chris, Kurt, and the other tall, young American boys.

Our group was really quite a good choir! Do you remember that we even sang on TV in Tokyo on a program similar to *The 700 Club* in the U.S.? One of the songs in our concert was the spiritual, "Dry Bones," performed by a quartet of David, Paul Wilson, Chuck Wanner, and Greg Allen.

In 1989, when Jim began working in Anderson, we all attended Park Place. This was a time of real transition for us and the two of you befriended us in such a caring way. Soon you began a small group that included us, the Spauldings, Liveretts, and Edwardses. For several years we met together monthly and had so many wonderful times as we prayed, sang, laughed, and of course, ate! You even started another small group with us, the Coolidges, and the Grubbses. It was amazing to see how many dinners and meetings you so graciously hosted in your home.

Margaret, you and David were so supportive when I had surgery in 1991. You visited me in the hospital so many times, always making me feel better! You will never know how much your care and concern meant during those very difficult weeks.

We had the opportunity to travel in your group to the World Conference in Birmingham, England, in 1999 and afterwards through Scandinavia. In spite of having two busloads of travelers in your care, you managed with great patience and humor! What a wonderful experience it was to see those Norwegian fjords!

David and Margaret, we are truly grateful to be among your huge number of friends. You and your family will always be held in our love and affection! May you feel God's loving presence surrounding you now and forever.

With love,
Rita and Jim Martin

What fun we had traveling to foreign countries with David and Margaret. David was a well-informed guide and surprisingly got us into the museum in Florence, Italy, to see Michangelo's David. There were dust bunnies on the statue's calf. What a grand memory.

The ever-observant David cautioned us to "watch the girls" (young gypsies) as we walked over the bridge. The "girls" didn't appreciate the warning so they pilfered a coin purse from David. Luckily it only contained some receipts.

David and Margaret always added sparkle and excitement to each trip. Love you guys!!

— Paul and Virginia Clay

David and Margaret:

Just a few lines to say hello, and to send along our warmest greetings and best wishes at this time.

We have such wonderful memories of several special times together... ranging from KIST to Phoenix...and more.

You are treasured friends, respected and esteemed servants, and we join with a host of friends and colleagues worldwide in sending along our love, our prayers, and our fondest hopes. May God continue to grant you "strength for today, and bright hope for tomorrow."

Most warmly,
Paul and Rita Jo Yerden

e have felt so privileged to know Margaret and David—what an inspiration to all of us. We took several trips with them and one to the World Conference in which they were leaders. David was so helpful—if he found something interesting to go to he always looked us up to be sure that we got to enjoy it too. We enjoyed so many things with them—shared meal time and Thumper with them. We have also felt privileged to have had them in our home several times for Thumper Club and especially enjoyed this last meeting. David watched us play, never complaining about anything. He seemed to enjoy eating some of the desserts.

We have one thing in our home

David and Margaret on an airplane

that we will always remember David and Margaret—we copied their clocks in the kitchen with different foreign cities and the different times. We will always think of them when we look up at our clock. It has always been quite a conversation piece with guests and we never fail to tell that we got our idea from David and Margaret.

It is hard to talk about David without mentioning Margaret—they go together. And what they have done in Africa will always be remembered by so many. They gave so much to so many unselfishly.

With all our love and prayers,
Meredith and Betty (Snitzy) Church

e will long cherish the memories of our two trips with you and Margaret to Sydney, Australia, and Birmingham, England, for the International Conventions of the Church of God. With your skillful leadership, the extensions of those trips to New Zealand, Norway, Sweden, and Denmark provided great opportunities to get better acquainted with all of our traveling companions.

One memorable incident I recall happened on our bus trip in Norway where we stopped at a scenic overlook and gift shop. I attempted to purchase a book as I recall for 13.50 kronor (Norwegian) and the cashier mistakenly rang up 1350 kronor. To make matters worse both the cashier and manager couldn't figure out how to issue a credit on the difference. Our bus was loaded and Lil (our guide) was pressuring me to get on the bus so we could continue on the sightseeing trip. I was refusing to leave until the matter was resolved when you, David, came to my rescue. With your encouragement we accepted the difference in kronor when you suggested that you could exchange the kronor for U.S. dollars received as tip money for our guide. Needless to say it all worked out well even though that gave us additional U.S. cash to carry on the rest of the trip. Special thanks to you, David, for helping to resolve a delicate situation.

Thank you for being a good host (and hostess) on these trips, and for being such a special friend ever since. Our prayers continue to be with both of you.

— Rod and Pat Whalon

Dear David and Margaret,

t's been several years since I've seen you, and I'm not sure you will remember me. I worked at Anderson University in the career office and went to North Anderson Church. David was my first faculty sponsor for the Career and Life Planning class I teach under liberal arts.

I just wanted to be in touch to say that many prayers, mine included, go with you. I remember you both as people who loved the Lord and provided a model of Christ for me when I was a fairly new Christian years ago. I pray His Spirit will be in you and with you as you confront this health challenge.

— Blessings, Nicky Margolin

Dear David and Margaret:

I first got to know you on a Mediterranean cruise in 1997. Norm Beard was retiring as the head of Tri-S. This was the professors and wives cruise seminar. My roommate was Alma Ann Newberry. We were both in college in the 1950s and forty-five years later were widowed.

Alma Ann and I enjoyed the port outings with the group that always included you two. Such fun to be around you.

On one such outing we were bound for Santorini. We docked and had to take tenders to the base of the island. When we debarked we had our choice of taking a cable car or a donkey to the mountain top of the capital city of Fira. Most of us "hardy" souls chose the donkey. When we arrived at the top, the only thing that didn't seem to hurt was our teeth.

At the top we strolled in pairs, looking in the shops and gazing at the view below. You two stopped at a corner store and were looking in a window. Suddenly above you there was a great flapping of wings, and a profound splat. The dirty bird had left his calling card on David's shirt and parted his hair. "What was that!" he exclaimed as we all surveyed the mess. It was truly a large mess which made David further exclaim, "That was no bird—I think the cow jumped over the moon!" What laughs we all had! We women began reaching into our purses to get our wet wipes out, and began to clean him up. That is, all the women but Margaret, whom we found later hiding in a store and retching her heart out. Such loyalty!

I met you all again in Birmingham, England, in 1999 at the World Conference. You had a group headed for Scandinavia, and we were with the Lockharts headed for Scotland, Ireland, England, and Wales. It was in Birmingham that David approached me about taking care of his mother, Pearl Lewis Stafford, who was diagnosed with lung cancer. I went to Sikeston that September and stayed with Pearl and Lester off and on for eight months. I saw you both several times during that period and learned about David's tender spirit. We were at Pearl's bedside together when she passed on to heaven. I loved all of the Hogues and Lewises and Staffords as I became a part of their family.

Whatever happens in the future is up to God. David in the Bible was a man after God's own heart, and you, David, are too. You are a gift to all your friends. Friends give each other gifts without ribbons every time they get together—simply by exchanging kindnesses and love.

Isaiah 49:16 says, *See! I will not forget you—for I have carved you in the palm of my hand!*

Love!
Berny Berquist Falls

Taj Mahal near Agra, India.

David,

You have been my friend for about fourteen years. Ken and I met you and Margaret through Tri-S travel and we quickly discovered we enjoyed being together. We were new to traveling and you were veterans. You took us to some of your favorite spots and enjoyed them again with us. You never let on that you might get tired of going to the Lake District or the Cotswolds "one more time." You unfolded history and geography for us time after time—you knew it all and the "teacher" in you just blossomed when we needed to know who, where, why, or how. We broke ground together in some unusual lodgings—the old Webster House

David and Margaret Lewis with Audrey and Ken Armstrong in Greece

Aukland, New Zealand 1995 — David and Margaret Lewis, Ken and Audrey Armstrong, Tom and Arlene Cappas, and Valerie Addison (Carl took picture)

in Grand Cayman and Simon's townhouse in Palm Springs. You got lots of lemons for Margaret by climbing up those trees in the parking lots.

Margaret and Ken always ran on ahead and saved the seats while you and I just meandered along taking our time. Margaret and I had lots of fun looking at you and Ken—and telling people, "No, they aren't brothers. They just look and act like it." (The gray hair, you know!)

Sitting under your teaching in Sunday School class was a pleasure and a blessing. You could draw things together and make the scripture speak. Your godly life through thick and thin spoke as clearly as your words in all parts of your life.

You were there with a hug and a prayer when both my dad and mom died and I've never forgotten. I love you as a friend and brother, David. You have not lost your radiant smile whenever we see you. My prayer has been that I want you back, but if I don't see you whole again in this life, I'll see you in Heaven waiting with a Rick Steves book in one hand, and eating a salad with lemon wedges only.

— Audrey Armstrong

Dear David,

*Y*ou have been on so many Anderson University trips with faculty members. The one in 1985 may be a bit remote in your memory by now, but Russ and I only got to travel with the 1984 and 1985 groups. I want to especially mention the 1985 journey with you and Margaret. While we were viewing displays in a museum in Germany, particularly the very large painting of *Night Watch* I think it was called, as we stood there, you made some informed comments about the painting which I cannot recall. What I do remember is your remarks about your favorite chocolate, Lindt. You were a good spokesman for it.

I recall a few years back when you and Margaret came to our Truthfinders Class and told us something about your work in gathering funds for the support of different missions workers. I am grateful for all you and Margaret have done for many years to promote missions. You have been a blessing to many in that work and to teaching students at Anderson University.

You are loved.
Velma Renz

September 15, 2005

*M*y favorite "David Story" came about when we were interviewing him for the position of OCI president. David explained how his father had told him of his prayers for David to be used by GOD as a special blessing around the world.

David did become OCI's next president and was indeed used of GOD through OCI to be a special blessing around the world through his service, sacrifice, work and finances, in helping build Godly Christian leaders worldwide!

GOD answered a father's prayer! Praise be to GOD!

— Norm Miller

David,

*Y*ou are a treasure to both Russ and me. Ever since you started attending the Church at the Crossing, I felt like we "clicked" with you and Margaret. Your passion for missions and your heart for helping people in third-world countries get an education is beautiful. I appreciated you for helping me learn about Overseas Council International and understanding what that organization did and what your role was. Thanks for all the times you invited me down to Greenwood for various coffees and meetings for pastors. Thanks for taking me by the hand and helping me learn! You both were so creative and had an ability to make your presentations so sharp.

It was a delight to travel to Costa Rica with you and get to visit one of the schools firsthand. We had some great moments—even playing Thumper was more fun when you guys were playing with us. Thanks for helping us to even plan the trip in the first place. You knew Costa Rica so well. I loved working with you when you were heading up our missions committee. You both know so much!!! It was good to have your help in putting together missions budgets, mission festivals, lining up speakers, and even speaking at the festivals in various classes. One class you did for us was "New Paradigms in Missions." Everyone came out of that class with a sense of awe. You stretched the minds of everyone who came.

Of course, the two trips to Africa were some of the best memories I will ever have. It has been a joy to travel with you, talk with you, and learn from you. Just to experience the road to Moses' house was an adventure I will never forget. You loved Moses so much and helped us to love him as well. Thanks for taking him "under your wing" and making his education possible. You also taught us initially a lot about the African culture. Thanks for coming this last January to speak to another group on the background of the mission there at Kima. That was enlightening.

I also will remember playing dominoes and various card games with you. You always had a great sense of humor and made things fun! We treasure those moments with you. You will be dear to our hearts forever. We love you.

— Russ and Maxine Jones

Dear Dave and Margaret Ann,

What can I say? Beginning with the Orient Choir, we started our travels. You guys helped to launch one of the most exciting parts of my life — Tri-S travel opportunities.

The memories are rich and beautiful.

David, I have mentioned this to you before, but you were my angel in Greece. I was flying alone from London and had to find a way to get to the ship for our Mediterranean cruise and I was really scared. When I arrived into the airport, I looked up and there was my angel. You, David, in your sensitive, caring way had come to meet me and lead me to the ship. Again, thank you.

As our ever diligent leaders, you were always reminding us of how to protect our valuables and possessions, and in Florence, guess whose satchel was stolen on the Ponte Vecchio Bridge? Stephanie, I remember a thief on the Hong Kong ferry that actually cut your strap on your shoulder purse! All in all we actually faired pretty well.

David and Margaret, along with Ken and Audrey, you always were so considerate of us "widows and orphans" when we would be at a port to make sure we were included in your activities. Thanks again for making us feel welcome.

I cherish the beautiful blue pendant that you all presented to me on my birthday on the cruise.

There's so much to remember and wish we didn't forget anything.

Your lives have touched so many all over the world and I am grateful that you have touched mine.

And remember, Margaret, Thumper is only a game!

Many, many, many blessings to all of your family and know that you are loved.

— Alma (Newberry) Powell

Somewhere in India.

P.S. David, do you remember eating in a restaurant in Bangkok when your chair slowly folded to the floor? The expression on your face was priceless! The chairs were metal, as I remember, with an "S" frame and were not made for Americans. And you're not a big guy, anyway. We had good laughs—you laughed with us.

This past July, Dr. Chris Accornero and I had the joy of being in Cape Town, South Africa, with Alan and Zelda Jansen. He was the President of Cornerstone College when David was with the Overseas Council International. They sent their love and prayers to you. How they remembered the many times you have given of your wisdom to them.

Chris and I also remember when David met us in Greenwood a few years back to explore the world of theological education and how we might connect with the institutions across the world.

Today Chris is an administrator/faculty member of Asbury Theological Seminary. Next May I will retire from Anderson University School of Theology. There are plans in the works for me to connect with some educational opportunities in other parts of the world. God is in charge. We can make the plans

Margaret and David

but God may have other plans. We do want to remain at God's agenda.

We love you David and Margaret. You have added to our lives and community in so many ways. Our continued prayers are with you in the journey.

Shalom,
Chris Accornero and Juanita Leonard

Dave and Margaret:

*H*ere are three occasions when our paths have crossed either directly or indirectly.

A number of years ago before Dave's Mom married Mr. Stafford, I had the privilege of addressing the church at Sikeston and I was housed overnight in Dave's parents' home. Your mom was so gracious. Your dad had been gone just a short period of time, and I could sense that she greatly missed him. I believe we talked about the piano contributions he made to so many Missouri congregations, and of course we talked about your wonderful family.

On one of those wonderful summer trips — a World Conference of the Church of God — you led us in Italy. We were on a short hike to one of the beautiful cathedrals, walking over a bridge. You both had just warned us to be aware of pickpockets, especially in crowded areas. About that time a group of young men surrounded Dave, distracted him, and I believe stole his passport. What a shocker for all of us.

Your time in Kima brought back many memories to Naomi, who spent five years of her life in that area of Africa, helping to manage the hospital, and brought back memories to me too. I spent five weeks setting up the Pension Plan Membership Files and writing a Plan Document for the African pastors. At that time the area pastors gathered in the small seminary building to discuss the plan. I worked daily in George Buck's office, which was known as the accounting office. My heart is strangely warmed when I think of the great and wonderful things you have accomplished for and at Kima International School of Theology. Your efforts will bless generations of students and ministers of the gospel.

— Harold A. Conrad

Dear David and Margaret,

*I*t seems that David and Margaret go together like "salt and pepper" or "cream and sugar." You are woven intricately throughout the fabric of our lives. Your leadership and assistance in the Tri-S program is profound. You have led several student Tri-S experiences and many World Conference groups. Our travels together with the Tri-S Faculty/Staff trips have been memorable. We have hundreds of pictures of our journeys to Europe, Africa, Asia, and Australia. When we think of you two and our times together, we can hear David laugh. His quick wit and terrific sense of humor made our days fly and our evenings fun. It seems that your desire was to respond to the hurting and to lighten the burden of those carrying a heavy load. We salute you and stand in awe of the missionary spirit with which you have lived your lives.

1981 Tri-S Workcamp to Peru

David, I grew up hearing about Ollie Lewis. He was an important person in my father's life. Isn't it interesting how our lives are so intertwined because of the church? Two men who were dedicated to the cause of Christ and His Church have impacted many lives. And now you and Margaret have continued this legacy of faithfulness. You have set an example of living with joy, with generosity and with faith for the future.

Please know of our continued love and friendship.

— Norman and Louetta Beard

David and Margaret,

*A*s we reflect on the wonderful times we have had with you, some of the most precious have been when we were privileged to be a part of your World Conference tours. The long bus rides were sometimes tiring and getting up at three o'clock in the morning to set our suitcases in the hotel hallway were not our "cup of tea." But the strongest memories we have are the fellowship you fostered through group worship experiences on the bus and the other group activities you encouraged both on and off the bus. We love you both and value your friendship.

— Herbert and Hyla Klabunde

David,

I will always remember the night before Margaret and I left for Kima International School of Theology the first time. You loaded the Librarian's Helper program onto the laptop computer Margaret was taking, unpacked the printer I was taking as my carry on, and made sure the program worked with the printer. About a year later Margaret and I were working in your garage to process books before they were sent to KIST and you typed the information in the accession book. Although you didn't go with us, you were so supportive and a help in the whole process.
Thank you for being such a special person.

May God richly bless you.
Mary Ellen Hicks

Dear David & Margaret:

*W*e have outstanding memories of our Tri-S travels with you and the faculty and staff of Anderson University. Even though Grada and David are first cousins, our close relationship began to blossom as a direct result of our travels together. We found we shared many common interests: our families, friends, Anderson University, Thumper at exotic places, golf, and varied cultural experiences around the world together.

Margaret, David, Ken, and Grada in Tanzania, 2005

David, one of the reasons we moved to Anderson was because Ken enjoyed playing golf with you at Edgewood, and living a few doors away made it more convenient—then you *moved!*

As time passed, your decision to attend Church at the Crossing and your involvement with the missions board at our church, caused us to have an enlightenment regarding the development of ministries in one of your favorite foreign countries—Africa. This would be especially Kenya (KIST) and Tanzania (BABATI). You exposed us to safaries, which we now consider to be one of our favorite experiences. You acquainted us with Moses, Frances, and Nelson—these men of God have enriched our lives.

We have always enjoyed being with you in your home or ours in Anderson, playing cards in many different airports, golfing wherever, worshiping with you in beautiful churches around the world, eating at King Gyros in Anderson or exotic restaurants, or just sharing together in our Bible studies. You are fun and interesting to be with.

Your lives have positively influenced many people around the world and have been a significant contribution to the church locally, and at large. Thank you for being a Christian example to follow, and involving us in your life.

We love and appreciate you both,
Ken and Grada

David,

I have searched for an opportunity to tell you what a profound influence you have had on my life and I have not had or taken the opportunity to say that to you. It goes back to the days when you taught Sunday school at Park Place and Vicki and I were in the class. And there was your leadership at Anderson University with the liberal arts program, the freshman seminar experience, and most of all, the deep spiritual life I saw in you as you went about doing what you did.

I saw the spiritual side of you when you addressed the guests at Christopher's wedding Vicki and I attended, the way you approached the lessons you taught in Sunday school, and the way you supported me at an altar of prayer at Park Place Church on a hot summer Sunday morning in August of 1995. The impact we have on another is often not known, but I wanted you to know that your life is a constant reminder to me of what it means to love God and neighbor.

Thank you David for being who you are and for making a difference in the life on one person...ME.

God bless you and your family. You are loved, appreciated, admired, and respected!

— Mike Eastman

David and Margaret — What wonderful models you are!

I remember the warmth with which you welcomed us into your new home in Anderson when you first moved in. We took a video of that grand palace. I was amazed at your humility and willingness to share your home with your friends. I especially recall the humble dignity and pride that David showed when he told about the chandelier in the dining room and the ladder to the books in his office. It impressed me in a positive way to see how one could be so dignified and proud and humble all at the same time.

I remember how you sang in the group of Christmas carolers for Hanging of the Greens at Park Place Church. You marched up that long church aisle, side by side, dressed in your Christmas attire, singing with great gusto.

I remember how you both led my children, one at a time and together with us, on Tri-S trips. How that enriched our lives! You first took Marleta to Europe and Africa. Then, when she went to Australia on a Tri-S trip, Margaret had already been there. So Margaret comforted us about what Phillip and the country were like. When she married Phillip, you both were considerate of my feelings.

I remember how you and our family all went on the trip to Japan, Korea, and China. David, you were especially interesting to listen to when it was time to learn about the Buddhist shrines we were going to visit. You were gentle and loving in your matter-of-fact approach to a volume of information, even when it didn't match with your own religion.

I remember when it was time for Bradley to go on a Tri-S trip with his soon-to-be bride, Amy, you were both there to lead them. What happy memories we have made together!

I remember your humor! At Truthfinders retreats, David, you were always anxious to help make the skits funny. And, at the pre-Tri-S-trip party we had in the basement of the Falls' home, I remember David dressing up as a bride. It was *so funny!* You didn't mind being the brunt of the laughter.

I remember the great knowledge you have, David, about church history! What a legacy you have left in passing on your knowledge to many students both in and out of the classroom.

I remember how we celebrated privately with you both and with the

Margaret and David at the Great Wall of China in 1996

Duncans. Last fall we three couples went to Beef and Boards together. We had such fun talking and laughing throughout the evening!

You have added to our joy! You have been loving friends! You have been wonderful Christian models for the world!

> We love you and thank you,
> Carolyn and Butch (Gerald) Miller
> Marleta and Phillip Black
> Bradley and Amy Miller

This is not so much a story as a thank you. In December 1991, our house burned almost to the ground and we lost ninty-five percent of everything we owned. We did have insurance, but David and Margaret contacted many in the Park Place Church of God community to collect items that would be immediately helpful. We appreciate so much their selfless efforts in helping others, including us.

So many times they offered their home as a beautiful retreat for women's groups and other groups from the church. Once again, they showed evidence of their sharing.

It is only fitting that we all share in prayers for both of them, who have modeled sharing for others.

Blessings and love,
Cheryl and Richard Willowby

It was 1983. I was in Sunday school with David and Margaret. My husband of nearly ten years wanted to end our marriage, so he left me and our two children who were five and two years of age. He was minimally employed and therefore paying very little child support, and I found a part-time job that paid $17.00 a day. Needless to say, times were tough. One day the mail arrived with a card and a check for $100 from David and Margaret. Oh, my! What a glorious gift that was. It felt like a million dollars to me. Even though I know I thanked them back then, I have never forgotten this unbelievable kindness and am happy for others to know of their generosity.

– Anonymous

While I have not had the privilege of getting to know David and Margaret well, they certainly have had an impact on my life. It was through David's contact that I have had the chance to work part time with Overseas Council International in my retirement years. What I will remember about both of them was the gracious spirit with which they approached me. Seeing them at work in several different settings convinced me that the Christianity they talked about was the same as what they lived. I especially saw this as they went through difficult times at OCI. On a number of occasions I had the opportunity to sit with David in his office and see him struggle with situations without losing that gracious, serving spirit. I will always be a better person for having crossed paths with these wonderful people even briefly. We pray for them often as they walk through this long and difficult time.

— Don and Caroline Gerig

David has a sense of humor that is infectious. He displayed that even as he was teaching the Ambassadors (now Sojourners) Class church history. He was a teacher par excellence.

— Guy and Gerda Perry

September 18, 2005
David,

*S*ince our families converge at so many points, I could retrieve lots of stories, but what Darlene and I want to do in this short letter is to thank you once again for being such a wonderful Sunday school teacher for the class we attended at Park Place Church of God, the IOU Class. Among the many images that we have of your leadership in the class are those of DAVID AS A CAREFUL STUDENT OF THE WORD. You always took the lesson very seriously and obviously did lots and lots of preparation for it. We always felt that when we went to Sunday school we were going to have the benefit of hours and hours of careful preparation. I recall the copious notes that you had before you that reflected all of that work. I knew that you always had much more information than we had time to process during that period.

But beyond that was DAVID AS THE FACILITATOR OF GOOD DISCUSSIONS. You knew how to get us talking about important issues, and you knew how to bring everybody into the discussion. We had lots of give and take and it always helped us to think more deeply about the issues at hand.

Also, we knew DAVID AS THE GRACIOUS HOST. You always knew how to make everybody feel at home and welcome. When newcomers came—and they often did—you opened the door of hospitality and many always came back because it was such a pleasant atmosphere.

In addition, we knew DAVID AS THE MAN WHO CARED AND PRAYED. When class members had needs, you showed that you cared deeply and we knew that you prayed not only in class but outside of class as well.

And yes, we knew DAVID AS THE FUN-LOVING PARTY MAN who along with dear Margaret laughed a lot and played a lot and helped everybody else to do the same whether in the Sunday school class itself or at class parties.

Thanks, David and Margaret, for giving us the very best Sunday school experience we have ever had as adults.

— Gil and Darlene Stafford

I have always been especially touched by David's humble spirit; he treats everyone so graciously, with such a genuine, down-to-earth spirit. He is a man who "walks with God." He and Margaret are compassionate and generous.

Our grandson, Clay, is a special needs child; at a time when our daughter Christy was consumed with care-giving and was discouraged and exhausted, David (whose office was close to mine in Decker Hall), slipped an envelope to me one day, with instructions to make sure Christy received it. The enclosed monetary gift came at a crucial time for her, but the encouraging words that he had penned in an enclosed note perhaps gave her even more strength and affirmation. She was overwhelmed with surprise and gratitude.

The timing was right; it seemed that David had listened to one of those "nudges" from God, and had acted on it! It was a kind and generous act, and could only have come from one who "humbled himself to walk with God."

Our friendship with David and Margaret has been a blessing and joy. We are richer because of their presence in our lives, doubtless a sentiment that you have read repeatedly as you collect these notes.

You are all in our prayers and in our hearts.

Thank you for inviting us to share these reflections; you honor us in doing so.

Blessings and prayers,
Sue (Miller) Spaulding

*H*ow well I recall the animated way you distributed Christmas gifts a few years ago at the Hubler's Pink Elephant Gift Exchange! What a twinkle in your eyes (I believe you had played Santa before...) and mischievous smile—it appeared you enjoyed every moment (even when you lost that lovely dancing flamingo).

— Bobbi Graves, for Jack and The "A" Team

*I*n the late 1980s Gail Smith and I were the co-executive directors of Women's Alternatives, Inc., a social service agency providing comprehensive services including shelter to women and children who were the victims of domestic and sexual violence. At that time we were moving to a larger shelter so that we could provide services to more women and children in need. We were raising money to pay for the facility along with trying to keep all other expenses paid. There wasn't much money to pay for furniture for the shelter. Gail said that she would talk to David and Margaret Lewis about helping out because David's family owned a furniture business in Sikeston, Missouri. She talked to David and Margaret and they said that they would be happy to help. Not long after that they arrived at the shelter with bunk beds for our clients to use. It's been a few years since then and I can't remember all that they gave, but I do remember the bunk beds and their willingness to help Women's Alternatives, Inc. and the women and children who were in need of a safe place to stay. And I remember their smiles and sweet spirits and their abiding friendship. Blessed are they who show up and help in times of need for they have the spirit of love abiding in them and they bless all whom they touch. For David and Margaret Lewis and their lives poured out in love all around the world and especially here at a homeless shelter, thanks be to God!

Amen.

With eternal gratitude,

Christie Smith Stephens

*W*e met Margaret and David when my sister and her husband, Blanche and Norman Steinaker, were living in Anderson and Norm was teaching at Anderson University. We then moved to Elgin, Illinois. David and Margaret just happened to be in school in Illinois at the same time. We coincidentally stopped to eat at the same fast food restaurant, probably McDonald's, on our way back to Anderson for a weekend two or three times. It was neat. They are a special couple.

— Dorcas (DeYoung) and Joe McAllister

Amazing Grace

Grace, according to Webster, is: "divine influence renewing and morally strengthening man..." I had always just known the word as a simple noun or verb, not worthy of too much thought until David introduced it to me at a time when that was what I needed in my own life.

We were together in Colorado for one of those chaotic times we now call Camp Lewis. Our gathering is always a mix of three generations, some with lifetime closeness, others of us, somewhat new.

My granddaughters Luna and Vega were among the new in the family. I found that time awkward and worrisome. Vega, a new baby, was in dire straits. She cried much of the time she was awake and could not tolerate being out of her mother's arms.

Meanwhile, David and Margaret's new grandson, Clay, was the model of tranquility. He smiled, cooed, and went from one set of arms to another without a flinch.

I felt bereft of my own grandchildren. Luna was grouchy, Vega screamed, and I was grieving. Nothing seemed to help.

That was when David said, quietly, "Sometimes, you just have to have grace."

That was all he said and it was all I needed. To this day, it is what I think of first when I think of David and his elegant way of saying little while conveying so very much.

Thank you, David. By the way, Luna and Vega are fine and someday I will introduce them to the concept of grace.

Of course, the plight of my granddaughter was never about me. She had severe problems with her ears which were exacerbated by the high altitude. So, I suppose, the lesson about grace had also to do with managing the loss of control one feels when facing the suffering of a loved one.

— Kathleen Cain

January 6, 2006

Dearest friend, David,

*Y*ears ago we decided to call our small group "Old Friends." It wasn't because we're "old," rather because we've known each other for so very long and we committed to each other that we would grow old together. On this day we are committed to you always, and to the memory of you. David, you shared with us your vision of meeting God, the glory of going home. Ah, how God revealed himself to us through you in those holy moments. You said, "I've seen it and I like it." Your vision comforts us. Your peace assures us to "be at rest." We'll see you there, friend.

Lovers of history, too, we were among others who gathered around you at every stop of our wonderful trips to hear the real story "David Lewis" style. You have always amazed us with that brilliant mind of yours, a gift to all of us. It's your heart, though, David—that sweet and good heart that defines you. Your compassion for the world and your passion to make a difference in the world always endeared you to us. We remember the evening you told us about possibilities of the gospel spreading to and from China. Your energy was electric and the "Light" shone so brightly through you.

David, even when you became sick and a man of few words, you called Chuck by name and always asked about Jarrett and Judson. You always cared for our sons and prayed for us. We hope our presence—hugs, kisses, and words of love have assured you of our deep love and commitment to you. We will miss you, dearest friend, and we will see you again.

— Janet and Chuck Wanner

Dear David,

The task of writing a few words of appreciation to you is an easy one because there is plenty of material and they are long overdue. Sylvia and I have a deep affection for you and Margaret. Our love and prayers will be constant in these difficult times.

I met your father and knew of his generosity when he was awarded an honorary doctorate at Gulf-Coast Bible College, about 1974. I was predisposed positively toward the Lewis family. Then in 1978, we both came to Anderson University and our friendship began. Ours was more a "soul" connection than it was an academic one.

During our years together at Park Place Church, I saw your pastor's heart at work. You were a servant-leader of the highest order. In fact, there was a transitional period in our congregation when I very much hoped that you might become our pastor. You discouraged my promotion of that idea!

One of the things I've always admired is your gentle strength. I've never known you to speak harshly or critically to or about anyone—even when you might have reason to do so. Your lives have touched so many, many people and we feel fortunate to have been included. If the world's people are divided into givers and getters, you are a wonderful model for those who would be givers.

Sylvia joins me in the sentiments of this letter and she finds other tangible means of expressing her love and appreciation. Until we are reunited in that place where there will be no suffering, we wait together in obedience and trust, servants always.

                    Yours and His, prayerfully,
                    Dwight L. Grubbs

Dear David,

I t is only a few days since the wonderful service of worship celebrating your life here on earth. As I sat in that service listening to the words and hymns, memories came flooding back to me as they have for the past several months.

When you, Margaret, Stephanie, and Chris first came to town our families went a few times for Sunday dinner at Ponderosa. I got involved with Margaret and Sylvia in working on Hanging of the Greens at Park Place. For several years Margaret and I did a lot of table decorating for events at church and elsewhere. You and David were always supportive of those efforts. After we heard you and Margaret talking about Truthfinders Sunday School Class we decided to visit the class. We are still attending all these years later!

In the early nineties we were on a committee with you and Margaret, Dwight and Sylvia to plan and carry out the Thanksgiving service at Park Place. Do you remember *Quantum Leap?* Cheryl Barton wrote a lengthy script for that service and you had the task of cutting it down to a reasonable size. As the narrator you "leaped" from scene to scene across the years as we chronicled milestone events in Church of God history. As we tried to select appropriate Church of God hymns to accompany each scene, it took the two committee members (Margaret and Avis) who had grown up in non-Church of God pastor's homes to keep you straight on what was or was not a "Church of God hymn." We both knew that if we had grown up singing it, you couldn't claim it as a Church of God hymn!

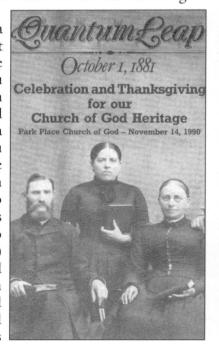

Quantum Leap

October 1, 1881

Celebration and Thanksgiving for our Church of God Heritage

Park Place Church of God – November 14, 1990

And then our small group was formed! We shared many wonderful evenings of fellowship, fun, learning, games, and certainly not least—food! We shared our stories and the bonds forged in those gatherings still have special meaning 'though we have not met as a group for several years. And how that group could sing! Often before we shared a meal we would sing before our thanks was offered. You often said, "We should get a bus!" It would have been a fun group to tour with! Remember when we spent an evening in our living room just singing favorite old hymns. It was a glorious time of singing and sharing.

After your move to Overseas Council International we didn't lose touch but our meetings were few and scattered. It was good to get together occasionally with you and Margaret to catch up and share stories—and photos of grandchildren!

In the past few months after your illness was evident I remember your sweet spirit and heartwarming smile that never deserted you no matter what the circumstances. We will cherish these and other memories in the years to come. And we will see you in a while.

With much love,
Avis Liverett

I first met David and Margaret in 1996. They wanted to know about Kima International School of Theology where my husband (Jim) and I were serving. During the North American Convention that year, David brought several computers for the first computer lab, and several boxes of books for the library for our shipment. Later that same year, Margaret brought the first of many "library" work camps. Over the years they have indeed been friends of mission in Kenya.

But their friendship with us did not end in Kenya. When we returned to ministry here in the states, we had nothing. David suggested that we pick out some furniture at a local La-Z-Boy store that he could order for us from the store in Sikeston. Ultimately, David and Margaret made it possible for us to purchase new furniture and appliances—at a dollar figure we could actually afford. Thank you for your friendship and your gracious giving!

Mary Ann Hawkins
Associate Pastor, South Bay Church of God

*M*y memories of you, David, all reflect the patient, generous, and selfless man you remain today. One of the earliest memories was during our seminary days (1969) in Turkington Manor where we shared a joint wall between our apartments. Scott awarded you "the most patient man I've ever known" medal for not being disturbed by an hour long crying marathon by your adorable Stephanie as a baby.

David and Margaret Lewis with Scott Lawrence in June 1993

Sunday nights after church were always fun-filled with games and snacks and many, many laughs. On Sunday evening, November 23, 1969, we spent the evening playing cards, eating popcorn and chocolate cake. After you and Margaret went home around 11pm, my water broke and I proceeded to go into labor with our first baby, Charis.

Our vacation together at Kentucky Lake was one the most memorable, with Pearl's Famous Fish Fry and lots of "scholarly goings on" by you and Scott.

You were such a good example for Scott in your unpretentiousness. As Margaret and I shopped you were able to find a clearing in the department store floor to spread out as your theological discussions went on (for you and Scott) endlessly. Stephanie, Chris, Charis, and Sally meanwhile had a ball playing as you two "watched" them.

I could go on and on with so many more memories, all of them precious, but I will simply send all my love and pray God's gracious blessings on you.

Love,
Nancy Lawrence

o me, David's story is one of faithfulness. He has proven faithful to Margaret, to his family and friends, and to God.

His faithfulness and love for Margaret are unquestioned; his determination this past June—in the midst of surgery and treatment for his brain tumor—to see that he provided a special, special birthday gift for her is something I'll never forget! With limited verbal and physical abilities at that time, he made it happen. How excited he was to accomplish this! I have seen in him a deepening love and appreciation for Margaret and all that she has done and is now doing for him.

His ongoing faithfulness and love for his children and grandchildren have

David Lewis with friends (clockwise from David) Margaret Webb, Martha Duncan, Jerry Webb, Ron Ducan, Jesse, Karen, and Paul Wilson in October 2005

been even more evident since the diagnosis of his illness. How thrilled he has been these past several months when he has gotten to spend time with them! And again, I see in his expression a gratitude toward Margaret for making these times together happen as often as possible.

He is proud of Stephanie and Chris and their accomplishments— especially in giving him wonderful grandchildren to fuss over!

David's love and faithfulness to God have been the primary focus of his life. At the time of the initial surgery and diagnosis of brain cancer, it was his obviously close relationship with God that moved so many people— doctors, nurses, friends and family. He has made it his first priority to demonstrate his faith in God, so that—as he puts it—God will be glorified. What a testimony!

David has given freely of his talent, time, and resources. The beneficiaries of these gifts are all around the world—his preaching and teaching, his time and service, his financial support—many, many persons have been touched by David! He has been faithful in these things to friends and family everywhere.

David, I'm glad you're my friend. Thank you for the many ways in which you've touched my life—you've put up with a lot out of me and Margaret! Thank you for being a faithful servant of God. Thank you for glorifying God not just with your words, but with your life...for being true to the end.

Martha Duncan
September 2005

Our memory of David and Margaret is at Park Place Church. ...They represented the most perfect family to us—a beautiful couple that obviously were crazy about each other sitting in church with two beautiful and perfect little children. ...They were enough older than we, unknown to them, and they were the perfect role model of what a contemporary Christian couple with kiddos should be. They remain that inspiration today. ...We love them!!!!!

—Randy and Joy Loyd

We will always remember David's teaching us how to eat chocolate. He would place the chocolate on his tongue slowly savoring all its flavor. Lindt chocolate was declared the best! David has made eating chocolate an even more special treat for us.

— Jerry and Joann Burand

September 16, 2005
David and Margaret:

I am grateful for the opportunity to share our feelings in this book. You have been a great support in my ministry at CBH (Christians Broadcasting Hope). You have come to the dinners and pledged your gifts, attended the CBH Conference several times and have always been so affirming and supportive in anything I did.

It meant so much to me for you to attend the celebration of my retirement at the Conference and stay extra time just to be able to be a part of it. You are such special friends with wonderful gifts that have been given to God to be used in any way He has seen fit. I stand in awe of the way you have allowed Him to use you these past few months. You have depended on His promises and found them to be true. You have encouraged us as we have grieved at your circumstances.

We have had some wonderful times of laughter, fellowship, and eating!!!! David, Jerry has said many times he wished he could be more like you — calm, with a gentle spirit, kind, even-tempered. I could go on listing so many more attributes he admires. Most of all, he loves you, as do I.

I wanted to share one story that Carolyn Patty shared with me about you, David. She said when her son Craig was in that awful wreck that left him with a mental handicap, you were so kind and patient with him trying to help him understand his college work. She said they would never forget it.

Thank you for your friendship and your prayers. Thank you for the glimpse of heaven we have seen in you. I will thank God forever for you two special friends.

With all our love always,
Norma and Jerry Brandon

Dear David and Margaret,

*Y*ou are so much in our thoughts and prayers these days, and also in our memories that go back many years. As I can best recall, it was a crisp October evening in the early 1960s. I had come to Sikeston to hold a revival at your family's home congregation. It was there that I first met you, David. You were quarterback for your high school football team. I can still remember standing along the sidelines with your dad, yelling for you and the Sikeston team. Boy, was your dad proud of you.

Jan and I are also very proud, in a Christian way of course, and so thankful for the special privilege of being both pastor and friend to you and Margaret. We got to know you when you made the decision to become part of the life of Church at the Crossing. You two are the kind of people that every pastor would love to have in their church, dedicated to the Lord and to serving people. You are both really fun people to be around, with a gracious gift of hospitality that makes one feel so at home. You, David, are a highly gifted teacher/educator, prepared, knowledgeable, and enthusiastic. You and Margaret are both leadership people who help create spirit and momentum in any church or group. We have experienced that strong leadership in your passion for missions.

Jan and I have been so blessed by your leadership in Overseas Council International. We remember the wonderful conferences in Palm Springs and Marco Island. Those experiences gave to us a new breadth of insight into the possibilities for the expansion of Christ's kingdom throughout the whole world.

Then there was the trip to Africa. Margaret, you put that together so skillfully, and guided the group as the professional that you are. That was quite a trip! We took to Kima International School Theology $10,000 from the tithe of the Church at the Crossing building fund to help construct a building there. It was there I first met Steve Rennick and had the distinct impression that he might possibly be the one to follow me at the Crossing. Then on to Babati where we attended the convention of the Church of God in Tanzania. Add to that the visit to game parks, the animals, especially Ellie the big elephant that almost stopped our hearts as she eyed us from too close a distance, and eating zebra and antelope in a restaurant with good friends. The final stop was visiting NEGST in Nairobi and having dinner in the home of Moses and his family. The whole trip was life changing and awesome in every way.

So you, good friends, have touched our lives in such warm and wonderful ways. Thank you for all you have done, but mostly thanks for just being yourselves—two really neat people who make such a positive difference in the lives of so many.

It pains us to know that you are having to go through this valley of suffering that is more difficult than we can even imagine. Please be assured of our love and prayers as well as the love and prayers of hundreds of friends all over the world.

> Your brother and sister in Christ,
> David and Jan Cox

January 12, 2006

Dear David:

Joe and David

*T*hank you for giving me the opportunity to be involved in your journey for the past several months and especially to be present at your beautiful home-going last night! Our weekly visits to Mounds State Park allowed us to quietly observe God's handiwork as the seasons changed from summer to fall to winter while the brain tumor was taking its toll on your body and mind but not your kind, loving, generous, and tender spirit or your delightful sense of humor. We had many good laughs about some very simple and/or brief happenings.

These visits with you taught me much about the value and beauty of life, friendship, silence, laughter, servanthood, God's creation and grace, a flowing river, a supportive community of faith, a loving relationship with a spouse and children and grandchildren, the dying process and the hope beyond it. Thank you dear friend. I will miss our visits.

> Your "buddy," Joe Womack

David Lewis as first grade president in 1952

e first met David and his family in Sikeston, Missouri, in the fall of 1960. We had returned to the United States for our first missionary furlough. David's father had expressed his interest in the new outreach ministry for the Church of God in Cuttack, Orissa, India, in the district and town of Keonhjar, Orissa. And Sidney wanted to share with him our excitement and plans for this new outreach ministry for the church in Orissa.

David was a sophomore in high school. It was during the Nixon-Kennedy presidential campaign. David talked with Sidney and showed and expressed keen interest in this campaign for president. Thus began our friendship with David Lewis and later on his wife Margaret.

As we have followed David's choices down through the years, he has always showed keen interest and commitment to do his very best in the road he chose to take. He gave that choice all of his very best. Most recently his excellent leadership in Overseas Council International for training and preparing young people for their high calling of service to God and His people in many countries around the world has been outstanding. It has been amazing to us to watch him as he served God with excellence in so many ways with his life.

Our love and appreciation for our friendship with David and Margaret Lewis,

Sidney and Jean Johnson

P.S. Sidney never bothered to ask which presidential candidate David was cheering for!

104

*D*avid and Margaret became our dear friends when building a house next door to us in Creedmoor Glen in 1991. Our home was started a few months before theirs, but we shared the same builder. Before really getting to know them I just couldn't believe that any two people could travel as much as they did! Little did I know that most of their trips had a special purpose and weren't just for their own pleasure or wanderlust. They were off to foreign countries and remote places doing the Lord's work and accomplishing great things.

Margaret also has a great gift of hospitality and I loved going to her house for dinner parties. Even a pizza party for Pedro's farewell was a grand affair! David was always a gracious host and went along with all the plans without missing a beat. He tried his hand at shoveling snow and trimming the shrubs, but those things weren't exactly his specialty, if you know what I mean. I marveled at his intelligence and his memory of names, dates, places, and events.

When he was teaching at Anderson University he was a fountain of knowledge and a wonderful professor. It was my great pleasure to help David and Margaret with house-sitting when they were away, except for the winter that the basement flooded. That was a little stressful!! I grieved when they put the house up for sale and moved about three blocks away, but we know now that it was all part of God's plan for them.

David's faith has always been evident and it has not been shaken in the least through these months of his illness. No finer example of a Christian man will one ever find. He loves his family, cherishes his friends, and most of all worships his God faithfully. I am honored to be counted as a friend of David and Margaret and I love them dearly.

> Thanks for the opportunity to share.
> Love you, Peggy Bell

Dear David,

What a pleasure it is to join with your many friends and colleagues in remembering special times when our paths crossed with Lewises' paths! In the early 1960s, while I was secretary of Home Missions, W. E. Reed and I made a trip in my car to visit Indian missions. He planned the itinerary, and included Sikeston as a convenient stopover. We got to stay in the home of your parents, and I discovered that they were wonderful hosts! Your mother was a fabulous cook, and your dad showed us around the furniture store. What a blessing they were to the Sikeston church (and to countless other churches)!

A few years earlier, while Dondeena and I were starting La Buena Tierra Bible Institute in Saltillo, Mexico, Brother Reed brought your dad to visit us. He was delighted to get acquainted with our students and the churches they were planting. The student pastor and his wife in Monterrey held services in their rented

1975 trip to South America

house. On the evening of our visit the living room was packed full, and people were standing outside the front door and windows. The spirited singing of heritage hymns in Spanish, a fervent message, and seekers kneeling, turning their lives over to God, made an indelible impression on your dad. The Lord laid a burden on his heart to help that young congregation have a church building. Within months, your parents returned to Monterrey as guests of honor for the dedication of a beautiful, brick sanctuary. Today, that church is one of fifty throughout Mexico!

Dondeena and I remember when you and Margaret came to Mexico

City with a group led by Oral Withrow. A most vivid memory is praying together in the hotel. Dondeena and I admired you and Margaret and were hoping you would become missionaries. After you accepted your teaching position at Anderson College, I mentioned to Bob Reardon our long-standing hope for you. He smiled and commented, "Anderson College works faster than the Missionary Board!"

We know that God used you effectively on the AU campus, and in Park Place Church. And now, for many years, both of you have rendered superb missionary service with seminaries in various parts of the world. Your investment in preparing Kingdom leaders is paying (and will continue to pay) great dividends. And your lives are an inspiration to everyone who knows you.

We resonate to the heartfelt prayer of Dag Hammarskjöld, and believe you do, too:

"For all that has been—Thanks!
To all that shall be—Yes!"

With much love,
Maurice and Dondeena Caldwell

Dr. Lewis, you taught the History of Christianity class at AU at a time when I was struggling to move forward in my foundation of belief in my spiritual life and felt like my Christianity was not connected to a good foundation. To my delight, your class became a great building block in my understanding of my Christian faith and its foundations and truly helped ground my commitments and beliefs as a Christian. I don't believe I ever thanked you at the time, so please know now how much I appreciate your commitment to use your gifts to instruct and encourage students in our pilgrimages. Thank you, thank you, thank you!!!

Gratefully,
Tamara (Caldwell) Magers

Dear David and Margaret,

Some years have passed since Ruth and I have had any contact with you guys, but as we have talked about your difficult circumstances, we have shared some good memories.

We remember the warmth of your home when Truthfinders (Did we ever find any, or were we always around the edges?) Class would be invited to "come in and be at home." Always great food! We remember your positive spirit and the strength of your witness to your faith.

Margaret, I remember the smile and supportive assistance that you always displayed when I needed information from your office at the university.

David, I want to go back to the early 1960s. Has it really been that long? I was a member of an Anderson College quartet with a western swing that lead us to your hometown where we were hosted by your family. When your dad entered the room, he introduced himself: "Hello, boys; O.C. Lewis and Company." A greeting like that stays with you. I've told the story many times over the years. He went on to say that it was a privilege to be able to host us, and that this was our home for the night. Your mom made his offer a reality. Warmth and good eats! As it was arranged, all of us did stay with you, and that was one of the best experiences of that tour. We all had known you as a classmate from the year in school, but that gave us the opportunity to become friends. Certainly, you have been a friend in numerous places to many over years.

Our prayers continue to be with the two of you. We pray healing and God's strong presence through whatever you face. Your courage has been a wonderful model.

Grace and peace,
John Albright

We most likely wouldn't know about "throwed rolls" if we didn't know David and Margaret. Long before we experienced the joy and wonder of such blessed bread we heard the story of the rolls. Word came to us via several witnesses that in Sikeston, Missouri, David's hometown, there is a place called Lambert's that you must not miss if you are in the vicinity. There, it is said, the servers walk around with all kinds of extras such as corn, beans, peas, and put them on your plate. These are in addition to the food that you have ordered. And if you want one of the famous rolls you just lift your hand in the air and soon a server will throw you one from across the room. The portions are large, the fare like home cooking, and the rolls just waiting for sorghum molasses that you can also purchase later in their store and take home for good eating all year long.

It took us a long time to get to Lambert's, but we finally did and we became part of the great host of witnesses who had caught and eaten "throwed rolls." We could join in the story and tell how we had been to Lambert's in David Lewis' hometown of Sikeston, Missouri, and, of course, we all know David. Later on we also went to the Lambert's that is on the way to Branson and that one in Foley, Alabama, and every time we went we talked about our friends, David and Margaret Lewis, through whom we had first learned about the glory of "throwed rolls."

"Throwed Rolls," just another kind of the bread of life, broken and shared in sweet communion. When our hands are in the air, David and Margaret, we can always count on you to throw us the bread of high friendship! How sweet the molasses of community, the stories that bind us together forever! Thank you for gifts eternal!

Love,
Stan and Christie Stephens

David,

*W*ell, friend, I don't really know how to start or where to go with this. You've been my friend for fourteen years, my best friend for much of that time. Aud and I have spent more time with Margaret and you than anyone over the last decade plus. And without a doubt, those have been the best of times. I thought about chronicling all of those trips, but decided against it, but there are some specific times that stand out. That first great trip to Australia and New Zealand and the spontaneous hymn sing on Sunday morning in the little church by the side of the road. Our great, but short-lived idea of trying to import products from Church of God mission fields and our presentation to the World Conference in Australia; the day on the mountain in Reutte (perhaps my favorite memory) just sitting and enjoying nature with good friends; the marvelous Lewis Thrill Tour to Costa Rica…and running into the woods (Sandinistas or not) to heed nature's call; sitting on the porch of the old Webster House on New Year's Eve, and riding the scooters all over the island on New Year's Day and Margaret snorkeling; the great condo in Palm Springs; spending Bastille Day with 250,000 of our favorite friends in Paris, Hilton Head…and crying and praying together as all of us hurt so much that only true friends could understand and reach out; seeing Scotland and England the first time through yours and Margaret's eyes…including the farmhouse in the lake district and staying with Joan and the bloke…and the last trip we took to Victoria and San Francisco. Some of our favorite places…Shipshewana, the movies, and MCL. These are just a few of the memories that I will carry for a lifetime.

David, what I remember is that on most of those trips you and I spent a lot of time driving to places where Aud and Margaret wanted to shop, and then sitting on benches, people watching and looking at greeting cards while they shopped, occasionally eating a Magnum ice cream bar. We also broke out in spontaneous song often about almost any subject that came up. I also remember cooking steaks on the grill New Year's Eve, laughing out loud at movies, Amish popcorn, thousands of Thumper games and the resounding "uh-huhs" of a challenging game of dominoes. There are a thousand other memories that are indelibly etched on my mind forever!

I have learned more about life and faith from you than anyone else in my life. As I have walked with you as a friend, you have taught me about love, about patience, about a spiritual journey characterized by the quest to serve God, about enjoying the journey...and about walking very fast. Your laughter, your

David and Ken - Sweater Twins

smile, your spiritual depth, your humility, and your willingness to think well of people will always be an inspiration to me.

I will never forget when you came to my office and offered me a position at OCI...because you knew how badly I needed support. You did that even though you were going through your own "hell" at the time.

Even our last trip together, when Margaret and you made a special effort in a very busy time in your life to squeeze in our Seattle/San Francisco trip, was a gift. We laughed a lot, saw some great stuff, and once again you gave to Aud and me the gift of acting like it was all new to you, just like it was to us.

David, I continue to write because I do not want or know how to end this. You know, one of the things I am the happiest about is that Kevin and Shelly know you and had the high privilege of being under your teaching in Sunday school. You have certainly had an impact on both of them.

None of us thought it would come to this. Somehow the four of us should have many trips and times together still ahead and at some point in the distant future go home together.

However, it looks like you are going on ahead to be the tour guide and prepare the place for the three of us whenever God calls us. Nothing has made me feel more helpless than what has happened during the last few months...but at the same time the result is that my faith and my desire for heaven as my ultimate destination are stronger than at any other time in my life. Selfishly, I hope that somehow God intervenes and the four of us will have great times ahead...but I want you to know that if it doesn't work out that way, we'll be there for Margaret and the Lewis/Armstrong connection will remain strong.

God bless you, man...you are the brother I never had and I love ya!

— Ken Armstrong

September 9, 2005
Tanner Street Church of God
Pastor Carl Addison
Sikeston, Missouri

Dear Pastor Addison and Tanner Street Church,

*I*t is an honor for us to write a letter on the occasion of this celebration of the life of David and Margaret Lewis. If it were possible, we would rather speak to you in person, but circumstances prevent that at this time.

We cherish our memories of our years in Sikeston and our friendship with many of you. In those years we had many fine young people in the church, and David stood out in the group. We remember him as very mature, and one who often spoke encouraging words to his pastor. At that time we felt rather young ourselves. Margaret was in the picture even in those years, and time has proven them to be a great match. We recall when David went to college and we were all sure he would do well there, as he did.

Through the years we have been fortunate to have continued our friendship as peers, both in the local church and in missions ventures. We often found ourselves working on the same committees. David and Margaret went on Oral's first guided missions trip, traveling to South America and up the Topojos River. That trip, and others, provided not only a missions challenge that was borne out in David's life in years afterward, but also provided lots of smiles and fun along the way.

Through the years we watched David develop as a leader in the church, especially in his years as a professor at Anderson University. He was respected both on and off the campus as a scholar and as a devout churchman. We were thrilled when we learned of his connection in ministering to seminaries around the world. His position seemed to be the perfect expression of his and Margaret's keen interest in missions and in seminary training.

We have been so blessed to have counted David and Margaret Lewis as affectionate friends at every stage of our life. We count their friendship as a precious gift from God. We join with all of you as together we celebrate these dear and special people.

With our love,
Laura and Oral Withrow

David holding his grandson Clay

*T*wo and one-half years ago, I was in St. Vincent Carmel Hospital for major surgery. Only from experience can one know how comforting it is to look up from a hospital bed and see someone you know who has stopped by just to let you know they care and that you are in their prayers. David was one of those persons who stopped by the day after my surgery. I shall always remember, with gratitude, his thoughtful visit.

Know that you, David and Margaret, are in my prayers during these difficult days. May God's grace be yours in abundant measure as you face the challenges of these days.

— Edward Foggs

Blessings from Kenya...

Dear Margaret Lewis,

irst and foremost receive greetings from the entire family of Kisii. We are doing fine since the time we left each other.

In fact I was very much shocked and astonished to learn that my inner most brother in Christ, David Lewis, has not recovered up to date. I and my family received the news with a lot of sadness, but all the same, we place him into the able hands of God Almighty, who is Alpha and Omega.

Surely sister, we are with you in spirit during this sorrowful moment when your family is undergoing hard times. My family is indebted to your family. I owe your family a story to tell—in life.

A trip you made to my home in Kisii, that is you, David, old mummy, and Rebecca is historical and will be foretold for many years to come. My elder son Obed remembers you and David well.

From our few days of interaction, I learned David and you as people with high integrity and instruments of the fine Word of God. People with a sign of mental health, who are glad when others achieve and rejoice with them. Thanks for making many realize their dreams in Africa. Let God restore your family for this good work.

Your family is a wonderful one of its own, you have a heart of uplifting ordinary souls. Sister have this in mind, that the world is a thrill with beauty and excitement. Keep yourself sensitized to it. Never let yourself get dull. Never lose your enthusiasm. Take heart.

I know and understand how painful it is in such a situation, but I would like to tell you that when you cast out pessimism and gloominess, amazing results will be demonstrated in your life and family.

Read this: 1 Jeremiah 33; Psalm 50:15; John 15:7; Philippians 4:4; Isaiah 38:1-22.

We look unto God to do a miracle to your family during this time of hard transition.

I look forward to seeing you back in Africa, to give a recitation of the greatness of what God has done to you.

Pass my sincere greetings to all relatives and friends in general. May God bless you. Thanks for now.

Your brother in Christ, James Mwita Okwena

114

22 September 2005

David working with Francis Kiboi

*I*t is with great love of our Lord that we can write to remember you people and to encourage you Margaret at a time like this, when you and David are facing a trying time of your health. Since we began to pray for you when we first heard about the problem that David is in, we have not stopped to lift you people to the Lord in our family prayers.

It is through this same Christ that we have experienced redemptive knowledge and forgiveness from the bondage of darkness and despair. Margaret we applaud you and pray that God will grant you much joy and fill you with His power as you strive to advance His kingdom. Your devotion to our Lord and your dedication to the needs of the church family worldwide have been an encouragement to many. So we have a reason to spend much time in thanksgiving for what God has done for us and for what He is continually doing through you and us.

May the Almighty show His favor with your lives. To you Margaret may God grant you His grace to help you go through this painful period with David. We are praying that the God of all healing may restore David's health. We are praying in faith and trust, knowing that God will grant healing and peace to David. To watch over him and His mercy will comfort and strengthen him.

God bless you richly,
Nelson Obwoge and Francis Kiboi

21 September 2005
Dear Beloved Lewises,

*A*ffectionate greetings in the name of our Lord and Savior Jesus Christ.

David Lewis, Margaret Lewis, and the Lewis immediate family, not forgetting immediate and distant relatives and friends, you are so central in the items of my devotion time. One thing I am certain of is the fact that our loving Savior will ever be faithful to His dear ones. I am patient enough to behold what God has for me in store as His answer to my solemn prayer fasting sessions that I have had for the purpose of lifting our dear brother, Dr. David Lewis, on the bosom of our loving Savior Jesus Christ.

Let me share these few insights with you beloved brothers and sisters. I borrowed them from the autobiographies of some of the inspired men of God in their confrontations with hard situations in life. The insights come alive in my heart whenever I meditate on the Almighty's gracious providence and unquestioned sovereignty despite the odds that we frequently confront in our day-to-day life.

- The assault of earthly enemies; the dispute of Jews and Samaritans; the doings of kings and counselors; the delays of years and centuries just seem so great to us because we view them very close. Viewed from a proper distance, as the Mount of Prophecy enables us to view them, they almost shrink out of sight—only important because of those large issues of which they form a part.

- We must choose not to fight the traffic jams of life, but rather to view them as opportunities to learn to wait silently for God and keep our expectation focused on Him. Dear man of God, let perfect patience be thy goal. It is the way the earth's noblest souls have trod. It is just a calm adjustment of the soul in all things to the perfect will of God.

- God deserves the praise that is offered to Him on account of His strength and His steadfast love, which assures security and triumph in spite of all odds.

- The existence of life on earth is so fragile and hence depends upon a very delicate balance of many factors. A small change can result in a total destruction of all life.

Tanzania, Africa — February 2005

- When things go wrong, as they sometimes will, when the road you are trudging seems all uphill; when the funds are low, and the debts are high; and you want to smile, but you have to sigh; when care is pressing you down a bit; rest if you must, but don't you quit. Life is queer with its twists and turns, as everyone of us sometimes learns; and many a person turns about, when they might have won had they stuck it out; don't give up though the pace seems slow; you may succeed with another blow. Often the struggler has given up, when he might have captured the victor's cup; and he learned too late when the night came down, how close he was to the golden crown. Success is failure turned inside out, so stick to the fight when you are hardest hit; it is when things seem worst, that you mustn't quit.
- Within this frail vessel lies the crucible wherein my faith is tested. The refiner alone knows how delicate is his task. The flame must be neither so low that dross remains, nor yet so high that the fragile beauty of the crucible is shuttered forever in its heat. And so steadily and gently he applies his fire; his only motive my purification; his purpose not wavering; his eyes fixed on the beauty that he will one day behold. Regarding nonetheless my present suffering with compassion; the identification of one who has also walked in the fire, and proved that

it does not utterly consume, even if it should include a Calvary. As in my fire I cry out to Him; and see Him walking freely towards me. I realize afresh that only in the fire are my bonds burned away. And I receive a heart poured through with love, His love to stand with others in their fire; until in that final purity; we stand together at His throne. (By Charles Sibthorpe: *A Man Under Authority* — the reason for the fire — a poem)

Finally my beloved, let us keep being prayerful and firm in our faith in the Lord even as we are confronted with such tough situations. Give the Almighty His own time and pace to work everything out in His omniscient sovereignty.

Yours sincerely,
Matthews Abijah Nyapela
Assistant Librarian —
Kima International School of Theology

Margaret and David Lewis and Margaret Watson with KIST students in Kenya

September 2005
Dear David,

*A*s you and Margaret know, Don and I live and work at Kima International School of Theology in Kenya. This college and the people here, including us, are not the same since you two got involved at KIST. We thank God for you and your commitment – first of all to God and then to doing God's will. God has had a special plan for you at KIST and through KIST for many years, and God has blessed this place through you. I want to say a big THANK YOU for all the love, time, money, and effort you have poured into this school! God has blessed what you have done and given many times over through you in furthering His Kingdom. As they say here "Bwana Asifiwe" – Praise the Lord!

I have several thank yous to give you:
Thank you for all the trips you made to Kima, Kenya, to be with the missionaries, faculty, staff, and students at KIST, and to bless us;
Thank you for sending Margaret to KIST so many times to work in the KIST Library and to bless us all with her love and presence;
Thank you for the groups you brought to KIST or encouraged to come;
Thank you for sharing the ministry and mission of KIST to churches, friends, and family back in the United States;
Thank you for your support for Biblical education in other countries;
Thank you for supporting men of God as they furthered their studies and training—Moses Alela, Nelson Obwoge, and Francis Kiboi;
Thank you for your financial support for KIST;
Thank you for praying for the missionaries and the ministries at KIST;
Thank you for loving this place called KIST and the people here;
Thank you most of all for loving the Lord your God with all your heart, soul, mind, and strength—and loving your neighbor (even in Africa) as yourself!

Don and I love you and Margaret! You have always encouraged us, listened to us, and loved us. You have invested yourselves in others, including us, with your time and support. I have benefited from that, and I see evidence all over the KIST community of your sacrifice and commitment. You invested yourself, David, in KIST, and only God knows how many stars are in the crown you will receive someday.

May God bless you and Margaret and give you all the desires of you heart. You are special to me and to all of your friends, especially those at KIST in Kenya.

With Love and Prayers,
Chris Smith

Hello Margaret,

*S*orry for your husband's sickness. May God Almighty help you in such a time in all ways. Remember that we are strangers in this world (1 Deuteronomy 2:11). Focus to God who is the only man or person who can't forsake us.

It has been so painful, traumatic that our tears will never dry up not physically but spiritually within our heart.

When we remember your fellowship with us at KIST, your kindness, loving, caring, honesty, and faithfulness upon your life.

God bless you.
Your beloved son in Christ,
Gilbert B. Kundu

Dear David and Margaret,

*A*s I attempt to write a story about David, I find that it cannot be done apart from Margaret for the two of you have demonstrated a lovely partnership in your lives and ministry. The words that keep coming to me when I think about the friendship that you two have so generously given to us are the words of the Apostle Paul in Philippians 1:3, "*I thank my God every time I remember you.*" I find it difficult, if not impossible, to contain my thoughts to just one story, so let me give a few word pictures that explain my depth of gratitude and the impact your friendship has had on me.

I picture the time:
- Chris and I were returning to Kenya from the States and you were on the same flight leaving Indianapolis. We were five pounds overweight in our luggage and Margaret ran to a nearby shop and purchased a carry-on large enough for us to balance out our load. Then, we flew on to Amsterdam and enjoyed the comforts of the VIP Lounge with you two. That was special! You went on to India and we went on to Kenya with the blessings and encouragement that you two have always been gracious to give.
- We sat at the airport in Kisumu and shared about forty-five minutes of fellowship and sodas before you boarded your plane. It was there that David and I discovered common grounds in trials that we were experiencing in ministry. I knew you two understood and would support me in prayer. How important that has been to me and it has led me through the storms encountered along the way.
- You both took time out of your busy schedule to meet Chris and me for supper at Castleton when we were doing fund-raising for KIST one April. You just wanted to "touch base" and encourage us! How we cherish those opportunities that have grown into memories.
- You stayed for a month here at KIST and we enjoyed Rondo together along with your lovely mother, Margaret Watson. Uno and Dominoes comprised most of our time. Wow—that was so much fun! Even more, you "listened" to Chris and me share our struggle with the

ministry at KIST which was at its lowest point emotionally. The prayer support you three gave us that weekend and over the next two weeks turned the situation around and now after almost a year the strides and accomplishments here at KIST are unparalleled.

- You brought an "Eye-Witness Group" to KIST in January 2005. What an uplifting five days you gave us! What fun our campus had in giving David a surprise birthday party! They still talk about it here. But, whenever I think of David, I will always picture him after that party sitting on the ground outside the Conference Center and talking with the little children. I saw the reflection of Christ in him at that moment. It took me back to a fundamental teaching of Christ, *Whoever humbles himself like this child is the greatest in the kingdom of heaven. And whoever welcomes a little child like this in my name welcomes me* (Matthew 18:4-5).

At the equator in Kenya, Africa

You are citizens of the Kingdom. Whether here in this temporal sphere or beyond in the eternal realms you serve as constant reminders to all who know you that we are blessed to be fellow citizens of this great Kingdom and partners in ministry here on earth serving the world God loves.

Thank you David and Margaret for being such great friends and partners in faith and ministry!

Warmly yours,
Don Smith
KIST President
Kima, Kenya

He Lived to Love and Care

*C*oming from Tanzania and serving the Lord in Kenya has been a privilege and honored opportunity for us to serve the Lord. This opportunity has also pulled us into the community of brothers and sisters from different corners of the world. We really thank God for such.

We first met Margaret and David Lewis on the grounds of Kima International School of Theology where we have to date served the Lord for about nine years. For us to have known Brother David, in our simple translation of the ordeal, is the reference to the message, Rest Assured. You have always been in our spirit and prayers.

The only measure of the stance that we can take, though with human mind it is hard to clearly understand and accept is to say, Let God be God.

We can only bridge that which seems to be separating by us turning ourselves to the wisdom of the scripture that stands true to every person

David at Kima International School of Theology – January 31, 2005

and in every situation. We confidently share this bit as we had done it previously with Brother David. *For I am convinced that neither death nor life, neither angels nor demons, neither the present nor the future, nor any power, neither height nor depth, nor anything else in all creation will be able to separate us from the love of God that is in Christ Jesus our Lord* —Romans 8:38-39 NIV.

David has been in our memory all along. His humble, friendly, and loving spirit stand worthy of emulation because he emulated Christ. He walked the talk and talked the walk, a virtue that we as a family admire.

Again we say, *The secret things belong to the Lord our God, but those things which are revealed belong to us and to our children forever, that we may do all the words of this law* —Deuteronomy 29:29.

In Him we live eternally!
The Mdobis:
Songelaeli, Timothy, Nita,
Linda, Kissa, and Daniel
August 29, 2005

Hi David,

*T*his is David Wafula, a former Kima International School of Theology student. I just wanted to say that even when we die our memories will live. You have multiplied your life in the lives of many people even if you rest with Lord, your memory will LIVE ON. God be with your soul.

— David Wafula

The more leaders I encounter, the more I realize how perverted the world is. "Good leader" has become a relative phrase. For many people, the standard of goodness is no longer the Bible. To be a good president and CEO to a multimillion corporation does not necessarily require one to be a Christian. Many fools and impostors have been regarded as "good leaders" in certain contexts. All these don't preclude the fact that God is still in control. He is still in the business of using the remnant to further His kingdom. Among the remnant (rare species) is my friend Dr. David Lewis.

Moses and David

Dr. Lewis has a good percentage of the qualities exemplified in Jesus Christ of Nazareth. He has served as a leader in various institutions. In all these institutions, he has displayed a transformational leadership style which has left him as a darling to many. His leadership is quite different from wielding power. It's a leadership which is inseparable from meeting his follower's needs.

My encounter with Dr. Lewis brought me face to face with a rare species in a postmodern world. He is a leader who puts others first by emphasizing the importance of followers in the leadership process. He has a strong emphasis on morals and values. He is a relational person to whom schedules are secondary. He is a humble man who exercises servant leadership. He is never obsessed with money. His goal in leadership has never been to gain something out of it but to serve those in need. He loves all people regardless of status, age, or skin color. He adores his wife and family. You

David and Moses

can verify the authenticity of this statement by interrogating his dear wife, Margaret Lewis.

Dr. Lewis has always inspired his followers, I being one of them, to accomplish great things. He has always understood and adapted to the needs and motives of followers. In him, I visualize a transformational leader and change agent who values holistic Christian ministry. Dr. Lewis has always created and articulated a clear vision for organizations. He empowered followers to achieve self-actualization and live a life God planned for them. He made others trust him giving meaning to their lives. He has provided transformational leadership through inspirational motivation, intellectual stimulation and individualized consideration.

I have served with Dr. Lewis in many contexts. I have never heard any profane word come from his lips. He loves his enemies and prays for them. David has no doubt impacted many lives. I believe he is among the remnant. I have a two-tier desire. First, that I live a blameless life so that I can still enjoy David's company in Christ's presence. Two, that his family members, especially his kids, will strive to perpetuate a sweet legacy of Dr. David Lewis. Long live the legacy of Dr. David Lewis.

In His arms,
Moses Alela

September 22, 2005

*A*ctually, coming to know David Lewis and Margaret Lewis and Mama Margaret Watson in the year 2004 was a great joy to me. They took me as their child; we had our meals together, talked and shared different views thus enjoying each others' company. This made the three weeks they stayed with me too short and I wished they could stay longer than that.

As we celebrated his (David's) birthday when they returned with the work camp in January 2005, which was so wonderful, it's when I thought of him being a model and wished to have somebody who can be like him.

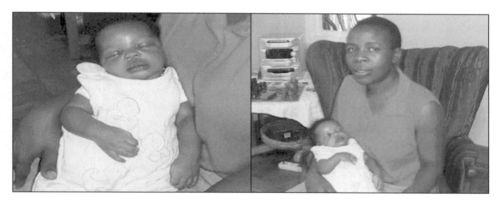

It touched me more when I was told of him falling sick and being taken for an operation. I thought of him being a special person to many people through his deeds.

His memories came back to me when I had been transferred to Maseno from Kima Hospital for surgery to remove my baby out of the womb. It was through God's grace that I escaped the surgery. I recalled the three surgeries David underwent and saw God's hand was with him throughout and through his faith.

This made me to think of calling my baby his name for remembering the year he fell sick is when the new **DAVID LEWIS** was born to me.

— Esther Anupi

Celebrating the Christ

Reflected in the Life of

Lyman David Lewis

January 31, 1945 – January 11, 2006

Park Place Church of God
Anderson, Indiana USA

Sunday, January 15, 2006, 7:00pm

A Giant Along My Path

Greg Bailey

Recently I was thinking about a book written by Dale Oldham. It was published about thirty to thirty-five years ago, and its title is *Giants Along My Path: My Fifty Years in the Ministry*. It is about people who contributed greatly to Dr. Oldham's ministry, helping to shape his life and influence the way he lived. They had become "giants along his path." If I were undertaking this project today and writing such a book about my life, one of the first chapters would be about David Lewis. God graciously placed me in a wonderful family, and because David and I are cousins, I was privileged to be around him a great deal as a young boy. We lived in the same community, attended the same church, and were frequently together at family gatherings. As a result, he became a "giant along my path" early on and has continued to be so throughout my lifetime for the following reasons:

Athletics

As a young boy, I wanted to be like David because he was such a gifted athlete in every sport he played. I remember David quarterbacking the high-school football team on Friday nights and watching him throw the most beautiful spirals with pinpoint accuracy. He could locate his ninety mile-per-hour fastball (it seemed to me to be going that fast in those days before radar guns were commonly used) wherever he wanted. And he had the most graceful jump shot I had ever seen. There are cases where you really don't want others to know that you are related to someone, but I wanted everyone to know that David was my cousin! He even taught me how to spit. In those days, the "right" way for any young, aspiring athlete to spit was between the teeth. I was practicing one day and happened to spit on the sidewalk. David informed me that I shouldn't ever spit on the sidewalk but on dirt instead. When I questioned him as to why, he said that it "breeds germs" if you spit on the sidewalk. So, to this day, I always spit on dirt.

We have shared our common interest in sports across the years, spending many hours sharing stories and experiences, and always consuming more popcorn than you could ever imagine. We shared the agony of defeat, watching together as our beloved Cardinals lost the final game of the 1985

World Series. We also experienced the thrill of victory as we watched the 1999 version of the St. Louis Rams win the Super Bowl. As Mike Jones made "the tackle" (as it has come to be known) to seal the victory, we were both so elated that we began whooping and hollering with such gusto that my grandson, who was not yet a year old, began to cry.

Intellect

As time went by and sports were no longer the essence of life to me, I realized there was more to David Lewis than being an "athletic giant." It began to dawn on me that he was simply the smartest person I had ever known. I watched and admired as he graduated from college and seminary; earned his Ph.D. at the University of Chicago while studying under the renowned church historian Martin Marty; pastored churches; became a college professor, and rose to the presidency of Overseas Council International, an organization dedicated to establishing and funding seminaries in third-world countries in order to train pastors and church leaders. But the most remarkable thing about David's intellect was that he was also gifted at being able to communicate with people at every level.

One summer our family made a trip to Chicago to visit David and Margaret. Our kids were very young, but David kept them spellbound with his vast knowledge of the city. He was their own personal tour guide, giving them fascinating information about buildings, landmarks, and everything they saw in the museums.

I also remember a powerful sermon he preached on footwashing while serving as interim pastor at Tanner Street Church of God in the spring of 1990. Toward the end of that sermon, he had one of the men from the congregation come forward and remove his socks and shoes. David knelt in front of him, poured water into a basin and wrapped a towel around his waist. As he proceeded to wash this man's feet and explain the scriptural commands behind this ordinance, you could have heard a pin drop. It was one of the most powerful moments I have ever witnessed in the life of the church. It was such a memorable event, this humble servant giving a real life demonstration in order to teach a timeless Biblical truth.

David has been a "giant on my intellectual path" by helping me come to terms with my own understanding of God and how He works through His church in this world. I can't begin to calculate the hours we've spent discussing the church and God's involvement in our world. As much as anyone, David helped me to form my own intellectual understanding of the gospel.

Friend

It also is evident to me that one of God's greatest gifts to me was the gift of friendship that He gave to me in the person of David Lewis. David is a "giant along my path" because he has been the best friend one could ever have. Time and distance have never separated us—David is one of those rare people with whom you pick up right where you left off the last time you talked. But more than that, David has always been a wonderful listener. When we talk face-to-face or by phone, I sense I am the most important person to him in the world. There has always been a connection between us, and I know that not even death will end our friendship because it is eternal. We will be together in heaven!

Spiritual

David, as much as anyone else, is responsible for the path I've chosen for my life. David has had more than an intellectual understanding of the gospel. He doesn't just know about God, he knows God. It is his personal relationship with the Lord Jesus Christ that has sustained him in these difficult days. He has been a "spiritual giant along my path" because he pointed me toward Jesus. I've been able to visualize the truth of the gospel by seeing David live it out before me. The greatest tribute that can be paid to someone is to acknowledge that they have great responsibility for your personal relationship to Christ. And David has done just that. Throughout my life, I haven't had to wonder what would Jesus do—I knew because I watched what David did. I started out wanting to be like David because of his athletic skill, and I still want to be like him. But now it is because of the way he has lived his life.

There is a statement about King David in Acts 13:36 that gives a simple yet profound summary of his life. It says, "David had served God's purpose in his own generation." That very same verse could certainly be written about David Lewis. Thank you, David, for being committed and faithful and obedient to God's call upon your life, and for being my friend. You are truly a "giant along my path!"

Reflections of Ron Duncan Concerning David Lewis

The Lewis-Duncan families' journey started in 1978. Both of us had recently accepted assignments here in Anderson, Indiana. Our children were of similar age, we attended Park Place Church of God and the relationship began. One year, Martha, Margaret, and the children took a memorable vacation to Florida during spring break, while David and I stayed here and worked. Many times after this our lives would intersect with family, work, and play. Laughter and joy were part of this experience as well as sadness and disappointment.

David and I on occasion would play golf. Our golf was not competitive with one another. Our golf was a time for talking. We talked about a lot of different things. As you all know, David had a wonderful mind. He could read a book or an article, and retain it in his mind and retrieve it when needed in the conversation. As brilliant a scholar as he was, he never used his intellect to denigrate anyone else. His conversation was positively engaging. He used his brilliance to enhance others.

David used his love of God and history to speak into the lives of a multitude of emerging leaders in this country and around the world. From pastoring, to teaching, to leading Overseas Council International, he was passionately interested in the development of called persons of God into leadership. His excitement in recounting the growth of an emerging leader he and Margaret had touched in some way revealed the selfless service demeanor so apparent in his life.

David had an adventuresome spirit. One day while playing golf at "Eagle Pointe," we came to hole number ten which is a par three over a waterfall, creek, pond, and rough. It is a beautiful natural setting that provides a safe play as well as the opportunity to go for it over the creek. Now most of you know, David watched his pennies and to sacrifice a $2.00 golf ball to the creek or pond was not his norm. Yet on this day, we agreed to not be wimps and go for it. I think on the second or third attempt we made it. When we did make it over, we gave each other the "high five" and thought we were professional golfers. This adventuresome spirit seen on that day permeated other more important parts of David's life. His love for the world that God had made and the peoples of this world was at the core of his desire to travel, see, and meet God's people. There was a desire to know all that could be known and to experience as much as possible.

David and Margaret demonstrated compassion for others. Even though today we are celebrating the life of David, he and Margaret were a team. They deeply influenced one another. Therefore, to speak of David's compassion, I must also include his helpmate. In our world there are areas of need that supercede the human capacity to address. David and Margaret in a quiet and unassuming manner just went about doing what they could — without fanfare, without acclaim, just doing it.

In our world, guys find it difficult to build meaningful deep relationships with other guys. David built relationships with several in this room tonight. The laughter, humor, divine example, and intellectual honesty demonstrated in David's life with us will truly be missed.

Memories can be valuable treasures. Treasures we can open and examine anytime we want. Thank you, David, for providing for so many wonderful memories and treasures.

David Lewis — the Young Man
Oral and Laura Withrow

*O*ccasionally you meet a person who lives with a special sort of grace that is different from the average person. He stands out in the crowd. There is an indescribable something in his personality and character that one cannot put into words. David Lewis was such a person.

Oral and I first met David when we left seminary and moved to pastor the church in Sikeston, Missouri. The Lewis family members were leaders in the congregation and were well-known in the community. From the very beginning, they became friends, as they encouraged and supported a young pastor and wife who had a lot to learn. At that time David, the youngest of their children, was in high school. We recall many meals at the Lewis home, many Christmas Eves in their living room, and many other opportunities where we had the chance to observe this family up close. We came to love O.C. and Pearl Lewis as mentors and friends. We fellowshipped with the extended family, as we raised our children. We soon learned that David was an extraordinary young man.

As was often true in those years, Oral was not only the senior pastor. He was also choir director, youth leader, and wore many other hats. He recalls that David was his lead tenor in the choir, as well as a strong leader in the youth group. Soon we learned that David was an outstanding athlete in his high school. Before many months had passed, we discovered that David had a friend who also lived with a special kind of grace. Her name was Margaret Ann Watson.

One of David's classmates wrote a tribute to David in later years. Speaking of his high school choir, he wrote, "The first tenors — that was a section that had its 'stuff' together. The section was led by one of the most popular boys in school. He was a role model. He was an athlete. He was a scholar. He was handsome. In short, he was the very epitome of 'The Right Stuff.'" The writer continues: "The leader of the first tenor section was [also] the class president." The person he describes was David Lewis.

Oral recalls that David was the quarterback on the football team and had the punting record that stood for many years at Sikeston High School. He played forward on the basketball team that went to the state tournament. He also was the pitcher for the Babe Ruth team that went to the Babe Ruth World Series. David graduated from high school as valedictorian of his class. With all of his skills and talents, he had a quiet, unassuming manner that put people at ease. He would be the last to tell you of his accomplishments. We knew him as a devout Christian young person who had plans to enter the ministry.

The classmate to whom I referred earlier came from a poor background and he felt he had few friends. In fact, he often felt that the "in" crowd at school was cruel to him and made fun of him. It seemed to him that there was a division between the "haves" and the "have-nots" in the community. Somehow, though, he felt that David was different. He listened to David and watched him closely. David seemed to take everyone's cares to heart. The young man never heard any cursing or judgmental remarks coming from David. He can't be for real, he thought. Was his behavior all an act?

One night the unthinkable happened. The young man's family lost their house in a fire and he was devastated. He wondered what the kids at school would say — how they would hurt him even more by their treatment. Somehow he made it to his last class — concert choir. When David entered the classroom, he immediately began asking the young man about the fire. "I heard that your house burned. I really am sorry to hear that. Was anyone hurt? Did you lose everything? Is there anything I can do to help? Are you sure everything is okay?" The young man was astonished. This guy was the class president and he really cared! In his tribute to David later in life, he wrote, "It is burned into...my memory. I will never forget the kindness displayed by this soon to be minister of God."

Time has a way of testing our character and the values we hold. It is apparent that David's life has stood the test of time. He has always been a kind, unpretentious friend who passionately pursued his dreams to make this a better world. Even as a youth, his Christian witness was evident to all who knew him. The Kingdom of God was his field of labor. We named our youngest son David, partly in acknowledgement of David Lewis's fine example. We would all do well to follow the Savior, after whom David patterned his life.

David, dear friend, we love you.

L. David Lewis
Reflections, Gilbert Stafford

*B*oth David and I are from southeast Missouri; our family histories are deeply intertwined. I first knew Lyman David (in southeast Missouri both first and middle names are given to be used) as Marilyn Gail and Donald Clay's baby brother. But since 1978, I have known him in a very different way, as a university colleague, a close personal friend, and as a fellow minister of the gospel. David was a warm-hearted intellectual who was a blend of Asbury holiness and University of Chicago academic rigor. He was a fun-loving soul who knew no class distinctions and found delight in all kinds of things, people, and places. It made no difference whether he was in southeast Missouri or in Southeast Asia; whether in the setting of his early ministry in Alabama or in his mature ministry in Africa, David invariably found the delightful jewels that were there and without exception the occasions for laughter. He was a world Christian. His devotion to Christ and the Christian mission called forth his best whether it was serving as Anderson University professor, or as interim pastor of his home congregation in Sikeston, Missouri, or as the president of Overseas Council International. His ministry was a creative blend of professor-pastor-president. *Professor* Lewis was always at the same time both pastoral and administrative. *Pastor* Lewis was always teaching important things, and administering well. *President* Lewis was always in both the teaching mode and the pastoral mode wherever he traveled around the world. For David, God, family, friends, and the Christian mission were his priorities. Worship, laughter, and history were food for his soul.

Last Wednesday night as I sat alone for a while with him in his bedroom after he died, I recalled a story he once told me when we were talking about the variety of settings God uses to bring about change in people's lives. "God," he said, "can use the most unlikely circumstances to bring about transformation." He then proceeded to tell about the unusual setting of his own conversion. It took place when he was a teenager in the Tanner Street Church of God in Sikeston. The pastor was Vernon Guttenfelder who along with his wife, Martha, played piano duets. Usually they played for the purpose of leading people in worship, but at other times it was mainly for the purpose of entertaining people. One of their favorite fun pieces was "Life Is Like A Mountain Railroad" (Words by Eliza R. Snow and M.E. Abbey; Music by Charles D. Tillman). Brother and Sister Guttenfelder would make the piano sound like a train chugging up a steep mountain. It chugged slower and slower as it strained to reach the top. Listeners found themselves trying to push the train as it labored up the steep incline. Near the top, it almost stopped, leading the congregation to lean forward in wonderment as to whether it would actually complete its journey all the way to the pinnacle. And then, with the people on the edge of their pews, the Guttenfelders would blast forth the sounds of victory. Sometimes when I heard them play the song, the congregation itself would burst forth into applause for the triumphal arrival at the top.

But on that particular night, for David Lewis the song was more than light-hearted entertainment. The message of the song captured his very soul: *Life is like a mountain railroad, with an engineer that's brave; We must make the run successful, from the cradle to the grave; Watch the curves, the fills, the tunnels; never falter, never quail; Keep your hand upon the throttle, and your eye upon the rail. You will roll up grades of trial; you will cross the bridge of strife; See that Christ is your Conductor on this lighting train of life; Always mindful of obstruction, do your duty, never fail. Keep your hand upon the throttle, and your eye upon the rail. REFRAIN: "Bless'd Savior, Thou wilt guide us, 'Til we reach that blissful shore; Where the angels wait to join us, In Thy praise forevermore."*

While that song may have some theological deficiencies, nevertheless, David heard the voice of God calling him that night to get on the gospel train, and he never got off. During these intervening forty-five to fifty years since that night in Sikeston, he has faced numerous mountains, but David knew that the track was secure, and that the fuel supply was sufficient, and that the *divine* Engineer was steady at the controls.

Last Wednesday night as David was dying, the sounds of the CD music that played continuously in his room (with hundreds of selections) could be heard softly in the background. As the family sat by him they could hear David pressing toward the top of the mountain. As the train climbed slowly to the pinnacle of this final mountain, the music on the train caught them by surprise in that it was another of David's favorites "It Is Well with My Soul." And then when he reached the top, and took his last breath, the music in the train, so to speak, broke into the glad and celebrative music of African gospel singers. Like the Guttenfelders who years ago had roused the saints to applaud the victory, how providential it was that Wednesday it was African gospel singers who roused the saints to celebrate David's arrival at the top "Where the Angels wait to join us, In Thy praise forevermore."

"Life Is Like a Mountain Railroad," and by God's grace, Lyman David Lewis made it to the top!

Message, James Cook
Text: **Matthew 25:14-21** RSV

Again, it will be like a man going on a journey, who called his servants and entrusted his property to them. To one he gave five talents of money, to another two talents, and to another one talent, each according to his ability. Then he went on his journey. The man who had received the five talents went at once and put the money to work and gained five more. So also, the one with the two talents gained two more. But the man who had received the one talent went off, dug a hole in the ground and hid his master's money.

After a long time the master of those servants returned and settled accounts with them. The man who had received the five talents brought the other five. "Master," he said, "you entrusted me with five talents. See, I have gained five more."

The master replied, "Well done, good and faithful servant. You have been faithful with a few things; I will put you in charge of many things. Come and share your master's happiness."

This is an unusual parable. It starts off sounding more or less like a business deal. It ends up, for the faithful servant, as a joyous relationship.

When you hear sermons on this text, the usual emphasis is on accountability for resources. What are you doing with your time, talent, and treasure? How well are you investing them? Those are fine questions, as far as they go. However, for the faithful servants, the parable points to the implied relationship in sharing the Master's joy. That's the good news in this text.

David said he wanted his illness and death to glorify God. He got the point of his life— to glorify God and enjoy Him forever. Isn't that the line from the Westminster Catechism? David would have known that. More importantly, he **lived** that while he was with us. Most certainly, he's living it now.

We come to remember David today, to celebrate his life, to acknowledge his incalculable influence among us. Most of all, we come to honor the gracious God who gave us David's life in the first place. Glorifying God is what David wanted this worship celebration to be about. So we come to glorify God and thank God for David's life.

In the parable some details are pretty obvious. We know who the master in this story is. We know who the servants are. At an obvious level, this parable teaches the lesson, "Be responsible to develop the gifts and talents God has given you." Myron Augsberger observes that it's unfortunate we've come to use the word talent to refer to our natural gifts. He says it's better translated "opportunity." The word "talent" came into the English language from this parable. The scriptural word "talent" refers to a weight of some precious metal, usually silver. In Jesus' time, it represented the daily wage of a laborer added up over fifteen years. That was a huge amount of money. We get the point. *Make the most of your opportunities. Expect to be accountable for them. Serve faithfully. Let your ultimate desire be to please the Master and bask in His joy. So, for those who are faithful, the parable moves toward a gracious, joyous relationship.*

If you want to see this parable illustrated in real life, look at the legacy of David Lewis. We all knew David to be a very gifted man. Those of you who knew him best, know how multi-talented he really was. But that's not what demanded our admiration and respect. We all know gifted people who have squandered their gifts. David lived life to the full. He maximized his gifts in countless ways. He recognized opportunities and lived in a way that demonstrated his accountability for his remarkable gifts. He understood that life itself is a gift. He understood he was given much, so much was required of him. But he gave his life and his gifts so generously that it never seemed like a requirement to those of us who saw him offer himself to God and others whose lives he touched so deeply. It was more like grace. David understood the stewardship of life.

Of course this parable can be applied to "time, talent, and treasure." But even more than that, it's about investing one's entire life, every part of it. Giving it away with abandon, trusting God to give back what matters most. Yes, David understood what it means to invest one's life.

David used his gifts, his opportunities, his *life*, to glorify God. He knew about making investments count. Some people are quite satisfied at counting their blessings. Others go much farther. They make their blessings count.

David Lewis was a good steward, a good *investor*, in so many ways. He invested himself in:

❧ **PEOPLE, starting with HIS FAMILY.** Have you heard about the 11,000 mile trip they went on? Nine weeks. Five flat tires. The U.S., Mexico, Canada. In a van and pop-up trailer. David, Margaret, Chris, Stephanie, both of their mothers! In her page of the memory book, Stephanie wrote that if they hadn't stopped him from reading all the historical markers, they'd *still* be on that trip. She says they "saw everything west of Chicago." When they got sleepy and he wanted them awake to see the sights, he played the "1812 Overture." **Boom! Boom! Boom!** I think I remember Chris saying he came to appreciate classical music on that trip. And they also listened to John Denver's greatest hits. Some of us boomers think *that's* classical music!

Get Chris to tell you the story of his baptism and how his dad came up to him afterward, gave him a big hug, and said, **"I love you and I'm proud of you."**

Have you heard Stephanie's story about the time she was in fourth grade and heard the other kids talking about Walter Payton? She went home and asked her dad who Walter Payton was. He told her Walter Payton was the governor of Indiana and Illinois and lived in a big governor's mansion on the state line. She knew her dad knew everything, so she went to school confidently the next day and told her classmates that she knew who Walter Payton was—and told them what her dad had told her. She lost some credibility at school that day. She learned to ask her dad, "What's your *source* for that information?"

You family members know the good times you spent with David. You saw him up close, and you know what a great man he really was. You remember how fun he was—and how funny. Tom Mullins says that genuine humor is a sign of the grace of God. And so many others of you who are here—David's friends, former students, colleagues, brothers and sisters in Christ. You know how he invested himself in you. Remember him. May God continue to give you good memories. And may your memories help guide you as you make your own decisions in following Jesus.

David invested himself in:

❧ **HIS MINISTRY, HIS CALLING.** He was a man who kept his focus. He lived a self-examined, disciplined life. He understood how important it is to keep one's priorities straight. Did you know David was a star athlete in high school? He lettered in three sports. He was one of the school heroes. In baseball, he was their pitcher. In football, he was their punter and then their quarterback. In Sikeston, Missouri, they're still talking about his seventy yard punts. He gave up sports when he came to college. He wanted to focus on his *calling*. He prepared for ministry. He graduated from Anderson College in 1967. He graduated from Asbury Theological Seminary in 1970. He was ordained in 1971. His calling took him several places. He served churches in various leadership positions in Kentucky, Alabama, Florida, Missouri, and Indiana. He earned his Ph.D. from the University of Chicago Divinity School in 1979. Beginning in 1978, he taught at Anderson University for twenty years. He served with Overseas Council International for several years after that. Many of you are here today because of his influence in your life when he served in key ministry positions.

David was called to serve. Some of us remember when the phrase "servant-leader" was popular. David epitomized what we meant by those words. He was strong, quiet, knowledgeable, wise, generous, thoughtful. He lived a self-examined life. He was a world citizen. There's a difference between being *well-traveled* and being a *world citizen*. David was *both*. Beyond that, he was a citizen of the Kingdom of God. David was a quiet leader who earned and kept the trust of those who followed him. He cared. He listened. He self-defined and stayed connected, as good leaders do. He took initiative. He was passionate about learning and teaching. He was passionate about training leaders in the developing world. He got people involved in ministry and mission. He demonstrated what passionate, compassionate, servant leadership can be. David was so strong in so many ways. He was strong enough to serve, strong enough to be humble. Most of us have learned it takes a strong person to be humble, a person who doesn't have to prove how important he or she is.

David was a man of integrity. He had his principles. Margaret was telling me with a grin how she and Martha would try to talk David into things. I didn't ask her *what* things! He'd refuse because of his principles. Margaret says simply, "He was who he was. He wasn't one way with some people and another way with others." What a tribute! David led by example, as all the worthiest leaders do.

David invested himself in:

❧ **HIS OWN SPIRITUAL, EMOTIONAL, PHYSICAL, and INTELLECTUAL HEALTH.** That was part of his stewardship. When he was twenty-nine, he ran to catch a train and was so out of breath that he decided he had to get in shape. So for the next thirty years, three times a week, he did his Air Force exercises. He lived out that part of the Shema that says, "Love the Lord with all your mind..." He was always reading, learning. When he worked on his Ph.D. in Chicago, he'd read for hours, then take a break by reading *Newsweek* or *Sports Illustrated*. Those of you who sat in college classes, Sunday school classes, or Bible studies with him, know that he loved the Lord with his heart, soul, and mind. That was a gift David gave to God—and to us.

David invested himself in:

⚜ HIS FAITH. Christian witness wasn't a job for David. It was his life. He knew how to pray. He knew how to wait. He knew how to depend on God. He knew how to rejoice in the Lord. He knew how to live gratefully, reflectively, *mindfully*, as the Quakers say. Didn't he cheer for the Cubs when they weren't playing St. Louis? If that doesn't prove anything else, it shows that he was a man of hope! Their small group met in December at David and Margaret's home. Audrey Armstrong suggested they sing, "It Is Well with My Soul." David couldn't talk any longer at that point. They were surprised when he joined in singing most of the words in his beautiful voice. "It is well...It is well." **How could he DO that?! It must have been what was deepest inside him.**

David experienced mystery. He was a thinking man's man. But he also had a God-given vision to live by there at the end. It came after his first surgery in Denver. There were serious complications following the surgery. Maybe it was a near-death experience for him. He had this vision that he told Margaret about, and then, later told his Old Friends group. Trying to capture the story is like trying to express the inexpressible. Janet Wanner was there at the time. She tried to tell me about it as well as she could. In his vision David saw light surrounding him. It was more than light. It was love. And even more than that, it was the assurance of God being personal. As David tried to express the inexpressible, he became animated, excited; his eyes sparkled. There was an invitation in the vision, as if he heard the word "Come." He ended the story by saying, **"I've seen it—and I like it."** There was an amazing sense of God's presence in the room. Later, Paul Wilson gave him one of those hand-painted Ukrainian eggs. The woman who painted it said she tried seven times before she felt it was just right. When the Old Friends gathered at Steve and Krista Meyer's home last summer, David was losing his ability to speak in complete sentences. When Paul gave him the egg, with its image of the Lamb of God, and blue markings, he came alive and started talking about his vision again. He said, **"This is what I saw!"** When he couldn't talk any longer, they'd get out the egg, show it to him, and he'd communicate as well as he could, *"Un un un."*

As Janet told me the story on Friday night, she said that David's vision seemed to open his eyes to mystery. She went on, "I wonder if that vision was what helped David have such a sense of peace." You who spent time over the last year with him, know how he could laugh at himself and his own increasing limitations. You know about his equanimity in the face of his own death. **It must have been his faith—and his vision.** Imagine having a vision and hearing the word **"Come!"**

When the end came he was surrounded by family and friends. They sang and read scripture and prayed. And then there were some moments of quiet. The CD player, set to random selection, began to play, "It Is Well with My Soul." And moments after that, David slipped away to be with his Master.

We understand this parable better now, don't we?

Yes, David was gifted. Yes, he knew how to invest his gifts. He made so many choices to give his life away in service to God and others. He gave, and gave, and gave. And in the end, there was the message, *"Come."* *"Well done, good and faithful servant. Come and share the joy of your Master."*

Surrounded by family and friends. *Secure* in the peace of God. And now, *safe* and *sharing the joy of the Master*.

I would like to die like that. Wouldn't you?

It is Well with My Soul

When peace, like a river, attendeth my way,
When sorrows like sea billows roll —
Whatever my lot, Thou hast taught me to say,
It is well, it is well with my soul.
It is well with my soul, It is well, it is well with my soul.

My sin — O the joy of this glorious thought —
My sin, not in part, but the whole,
Is nailed to the cross, and I bear it no more:
Praise the Lord, praise the Lord, O my soul!
It is well with my soul, It is well, it is well with my soul.

And, Lord, haste the day when my faith shall be sight,
The clouds be rolled back as a scroll:
The trump shall resound and the Lord shall descend,
"Even so" — it is well with my soul.
It is well with my soul, It is well, it is well with my soul.